A Veteran's Guide to Higher Education

Surviving the Transition from Military Service to the Academic Environment

Mike Cubbage

ISBN: 978-1-4834-6151-9 (sc)
ISBN: 978-1-4834-6149-6 (hc)
ISBN: 978-1-4834-6150-2 (e)

Library of Congress Control Number: 2016918861

Because of the dynamic nature of the Internet, any web addresses or links contained in this book may have changed since publication and may no longer be valid. The views expressed in this work are solely those of the author and do not necessarily reflect the views of the publisher, and the publisher hereby disclaims any responsibility for them.

Any people depicted in stock imagery provided by Thinkstock are models, and such images are being used for illustrative purposes only. Certain stock imagery © Thinkstock.

Lulu Publishing Services rev. date: 11/30/2016

To Alecxander Anthony Silva
September 30, 1990—June 30, 2016
See you in Valhalla, brother.

Contents

Preface

I WROTE THIS BOOK AFTER being approached by many of my military colleagues throughout my career who saw that I was able to balance a military career with an academic one. They saw me at times struggle both mentally, while dealing with issues such as PSTD and TBI; socially, in dealing with a demographic I was no longer used to dealing with after having spent a significant time in the military; and physically due to my injuries.

I also ran into financial and medical issues that made things hard on me as a single guy with a limited support system, and at times I felt all alone in trying to succeed where I knew I needed help.

After attending almost half a dozen colleges, both brick and mortar and through online programs, I have become an expert in navigating the academic labyrinth. From initial application processes all the way to graduation, I have made it a mission of mine to devise a system that I know will work for all transitioning service members.

I have been called on time and time again by professors both at the undergraduate and graduate level to take under my wing veterans who exhibited many of the same attributes I did when I started my academic mission. I helped to show them that although it is a difficult process, it is nothing that we can't handle, and with a little proper planning and simple implementation of our already acquired military skill sets, there was no reason we can't only survive but thrive in this environment.

I have written several journal articles and scholarly papers in regards to this process, have been interviewed in print and radio broadcasts on this subject, spoken at national symposiums, and was finally cornered by enough of my friends and colleagues to really get this out to all of you via a survival guide in order for you to capitalize on my successes and learn from my failures.

I have devoted my professional career now to seeing to it that veterans transition more smoothly than they have in the past, both in the academic environment as well as the professional arena through my publications, blog, and involvement in veteran startups intent on veteran advocacy.

This is now where my professional knowledge, expertise, and passion lies.

Acknowledgments

I THANK MY BROTHER IAN, who has always had my back, has never ceased to impress and amaze me, stays true to his principles and resolve, and saved lives on the battlefield. He is a true American hero and an inspiration to those who refuse to relent or waiver in the face of poor leadership.

To my father who has always been a role model and a hero to me as well as others, a man whose moral compass is true, tested, and unwavering, someone I strive to emulate and stand proud to carry his name, a man who told me that there was nothing I could not accomplish and through thick and thin saw to it that I stayed the course.

To my mother who always saw to it that I refused to settle for anything less than what I was fully capable of and demanded nothing but the best from me in everything I set out to accomplish.

To my infantry brothers of the 101st, as well as soldiers, sailors, marines, coasties, and airmen I had the pleasure and honor to serve beside.

To my ROTC crew that made my college experience more than bearable and have become exceptional leaders across the Army, Navy, Marine Corps, and Coast Guard.

To those who paved the way for us and those who will carry the flag forward when we are gone.

And to those who paid the ultimate sacrifice, you will never be forgotten.

To my friends who have always supported me no matter what crazy endeavor I was about to pursue.

I would also like to thank my leaders who saw something in me, put up with my shit, and pushed me forward, to my soldiers who made it easy for me to be a leader, and to those professors who took a personal interest in seeing to it that I achieve my objective.

I thank you all.

Introduction

AFTER A CAREER IN the armed services, service members often find the transition back to civilian life to be a laborious process. The changes in the daily schedule, the chaos of dealing with civilians with a less than disciplined way of life, and the simple logistics associated with establishing personal and family healthcare and education, as well as other issues, can make this a daunting endeavor—not to mention the journey toward a civilian career that keeps the service member engaged, productive, and happy. This is the road we all must travel when we leave the service.

But we are used to traveling the road less traveled. In fact, we often make our own roads, and stepping into the academic environment after years of service can require us to bulldoze our own path. There have been those who have succeeded before us and have carved out trails and offered words of advice and support, but it has not been until now that our brothers and sisters have come back in such large numbers attempting to brave the scholarly battlefield. From an associate's degree all the way to a doctorate, we are filling the ranks of the student populations from coast to coast—this is great.

A soldier, sailor, marine, and airman is a well-oiled machine, disciplined, and ready to tackle any task with vigor and determination. An *educated* soldier, sailor, marine, or airman, is truly the .001 percent and a mental and physical phenome. I applaud you for taking the step toward completing your next mission, receiving higher education. You will find that this will become a force multiplier for you and will propel you into future successes that your service alone may not have been able to provide.

This will not be a short or easy process, but you already know that, and you are already prepared, for you have been in the suck and are some of the best our nation has to offer. View this book as a guide, a field manual to provide you with the necessary information that you will need to navigate your next course of action. I certainly wish I had something like this to help guide me when I got out.

With that being said, know that field manuals are never the be-all and end-all, and your own supplemental insight will make this field manual all that much more productive to you as you apply your own knowledge, experiences, and practices to the ones I have provided for you here. At the end of the day you make the decisions, you walk the walk, and when you accomplish this mission, you'll have another important badge for your chest.

Good luck and God speed.

Chapter 1

Admission

THE ADMISSION PROCESS CAN be an intimidating animal. From application deadlines to standardized testing to figuring out the labyrinth that is financial aid. But like we are used to hearing, "It's been done." In the following chapter, you will find a list of standardized tests that you should become familiar with if you decide to pursue your higher education. Oftentimes bases and posts offer these tests through their education centers as a courtesy to service members (SM) during their out-processing process.

Oftentimes SMs do not take advantage of these free yet otherwise expensive opportunities because they are in a rush to get out, don't want to have to take another "friggin" test, or simply don't think they will be pursuing higher education when they get out. It is quite often the case that SMs don't realize until they have been out for some time and familiarize themselves with the requirements of success in the civilian world that they should have taken advantage of these opportunities when they were presented to them at no cost, oftentimes with guidance, tutoring, study assistance, and free study materials.

Many SMs also do not know that these programs are available to them during their terms of service through their academic centers and usually simply require command approval to participate. So instead of "boozin' it up" *every* night, you can spend at least a couple during the week after work getting in a couple study courses to prepare for these tests so that they don't seem to come at you all at once upon out-processing.

SAT

The SAT is the Standard Aptitude Test and is usually given in high school to juniors and seniors preparing for entrance into two- and four-year-college degree programs. Often referred to as the "college boards" the SAT is designed to measure an applicant's aptitude or projected success rate in a given academic environment. All colleges accept the SAT, although as of late it seems there has been some trend in some colleges not requiring it.

The SAT is given seven times a year and you must register with the College Board via their website: https://sat.collegeboard.org/ SAT/next-steps-toward-college?s_kwcid=AL!4330!10!3106072374! 14977004344&ef_id=UvgVlgAAAc0t4D4v:20150815225909:s.

The SAT costs about fifty-five dollars to take, and you must preregister. Your education center can help you through this process if you choose to do this before you end your term of service. This is your best option, as your unit will often not only cover the cost of the registration fee but will also cover the costs of prep courses associated with this test.

The SAT tests your reading, writing, and mathematics skills. It does this through sections that include reading comprehension, grammar error recognition, and short essays. The math portion primarily includes questions regarding basic arithmetic, algebra, geometry, statistics, and probability. There are ten sections totaling three hours and forty-five minutes. You will also have several breaks throughout the test so as not to "burn your brain out."

The SAT also offers subject specific add on tests that you have the option to take to show colleges that you have a particular proficiency in a certain area. Some of these areas include literature, biology, chemistry, German, Spanish, physics, etc. So if you were an engineer in the service, it may behoove you to take the additional physics add-on if you plan to pursue a career in engineering after service, or one of the language add-ons if you happened to be a linguist and plan on staying with that course of action throughout your higher education and subsequent career choice.

In order to prepare for the SAT (which is recommended), you have several options. There are several companies that offer study guides and study courses that can aid you in achieving your highest grade on the SAT, and your education center can help and maybe even provide you with the materials for these. Remember, though, that once you leave service, these courses can come at a hefty price, some costing thousands of dollars.

But when it's all said and done, it is important to note that the SAT, although an important part of the application process, is not the only deciding factor. Do not get discouraged if you do not achieve the score you desire. Colleges use the SAT as one of many factors to determine admissions. Your high school grades, military service, community service, college interview, college essay, as well as several other factors influence colleges in regards to the admissions process.

LSAT

The LSAT is the Law School Admission Test. It is what you will take after receiving your four-year degree if you decide to pursue a juris doctor or law degree. Much like the SAT, the LSAT is one tool used to measure the projected success of a future law student and is not the only deciding factor in gaining admission to law school.

The LSAT is designed to measure a student's analytical skills, and the test is comprised mostly of puzzles and logic games that the test taker must solve. The multiple-choice sections are broken down into reading comprehension, analytical reasoning, and logical reasoning tests. The test is comprised of five thirty-five-minute multiple-choice sections and one thirty-five-minute writing sample. The writing sample is not graded. Rather, it is simply an example to law schools of how you write. You will also have breaks between these sections.

The test is given eight times a year, and much like the SAT you must preregister through LSAC. Their website is http://www.lsac.org/jd/lsat/. Once again, your education center should have information and maybe even materials to help you study for this test. It is highly recommended that you take this test seriously and put forth serious effort in studying, as law school admissions are highly competitive, especially currently. I certainly shot myself in the foot in this area.

Many of the same companies that offer SAT prep offer LSAT prep as well. These courses are very expensive, ranging in the thousands depending on the chosen prep course. The cost of the LSAT is $175.00, with a credential assembly service fee of $170.00. This credential assembly fee applies to LSAC, which organizes your entire law school admissions packet including but not limited to your LSAT scores, college transcripts, and recommendations into a digital portfolio, making it easier to send to prospective law schools of your choice. Beware, though, that deadlines are very important here. Missing one registration deadline can cost you an extra ninety dollars.

MCAT

The MCAT is the Medical College Admission Test. This is the test you will take upon completion of your four-year degree in order to apply to medical school. Registration for this test takes place on this site: https://www.aamc.org/students/applying/mcat/. The MCAT is an entirely multiple-choice exam designed to measure an applicant's knowledge of natural, behavioral, and social science concepts. It also measures critical and analytical skills necessary for the study of medicine. Much like the other two exams, it is only given a few times a year, and more information can be viewed on the aforementioned website.

GRE

The GRE is the Graduate Record Exam and is the exam you will take upon completion of a four-year degree in order to move on to a master of arts or master of science program, although it is important to note that not all graduate schools require this exam—that is something important to think about in terms of expediency.

There are many online programs available to SMs that can be completed online after work or even during downtime which rival some brick and mortar institutions. American Military University is a great example of an institution that offers master's degrees and is particularly in tune with the needs of SMs (i.e., deployments, field time, etc.).

They also offer courses that are more in line with what many commanders seek in their junior leaders—"wealth of knowledge." Courses in international relations, counterterrorism, organized crime, investigations, and other areas more pertinent to our line of work also carry over into the civilian world if you chose to work for local law enforcement, as a DOD civilian, or even for one of the "three-letter agencies."

Oftentimes units that see junior leaders, senior leaders, and senior NCOs who already have a four-year degree but desire to achieve an MA or MS will provide tuition assistance to those individuals oftentimes making tuition much more affordable. This is another opportunity often passed up by many in our ranks, and it is a shame. Utilize it if you have the opportunity. But I digress.

The GRE tests verbal reasoning, quantitative reasoning, and analytical writing. This test is given much more frequently, as much as once a month with computer access. This test costs $175.00, but you must remember to register on time. Much like the other tests there are supplemental study materials, but unlike the other tests, the GRE through http://www.ets.org/gre/revised_general/ offers free study materials that I hear from colleagues suffice.

GMAT

The GMAT is the Graduate Management Admission Test. Another graduate school–level test, this test gears itself toward those interested in pursuing a higher degree in a business, such as an MBA. Although many graduate school applicants tend to take both exams, the GMAT is often a requirement for most upper-level business schools. The GMAT, much like the GRE, is given quite often and costs $250.00 to register. Much like the GRE, the GMAT has plenty of expensive prep courses that you can chose to take for a fee, but the official registration site, www.mba.com, also offers free materials that, once again, I have been told by colleagues suffice.

Converting Military Training to Academic Credits

Many SMs do not realize that while out-processing, and even after, they can convert some of their military service and courses into college credits. By receiving your joint services transcripts, you can leave the service with an official document to hand to your school upon acceptance. You can access JST here: https://jst.doded.mil.

I, for one, didn't know this until I had completed my undergraduate degree, and I wish I would have. Things like airborne school, air assault, or Ranger school, even basic training, can easily be transferred to physical education credits. Some colleges and universities that require these as mandatory credits for graduation often have no problem recognizing an SM's physical accomplishments during their time of service by allowing them to bow out of those courses that they feel the SM may have already completed through their military service.

Other courses such as NCO development courses and technical courses such as track mechanic, demolition diver, and other advanced individual training courses can be applied to your higher education, even if it is only to shave off a prerequisite for a higher course or allow you to CLEP test out of a course rather than have to pay for an entire semester to sit and learn what you already know.

So make sure to keep your DD-214 up to date and do not rush out of out-processing without making sure that all of your schools and qualifications are listed and up to date. Your education center will help you with this, and you can actually be proactive throughout your career by ensuring that your schools and training are added to your JST while still in service. Once again the education center is your friend here. I can't even count how many times I visited our post center and was amazed at how underutilized it was and how eager the civilians there were to help in any way.

The Importance of an "I-Love-Me Book"

I always stress the importance of keeping an "I-love-me book," or a file with *every* single shred of paper the army ever gave me, including profiles, school diplomas, jump logs, *everything*, just in case I needed it in the future, and I cannot tell you how many times it has saved me in a pinch.

I have everything in there from my first target qualification as a private in basic training to my DD-214 and everything in between. I really cannot stress enough how important it is to keep all of this stuff. Too many times has one of my soldiers come up to me, asking for my help with this process and when asked where his orders or documentation to validate his claim are he just looked at me with a blank stare. If you don't have orders for it in hand, it isn't yours or you didn't do it in the eyes of Mother DOD.

I learned this lesson early in my career as a private, but I was reminded six years later after being commissioned as a second lieutenant. Upon arriving at my new duty station as a brand-new "butter bar," I was checking into S-1 personnel when the civilian behind the counter looked at my chest and said in a very cocky and quite rude manner, "You ain't airborne!"

I was taken aback, as I'd been a paratrooper for six years, and I replied quite frankly in the same tone, "Uh, my wings say I am."

She then explained to me that my new officer record brief had no record of me ever completing airborne school, so she asked me if I had my airborne orders (from six years ago—serious, like I carry them in my pocket).

So I explained to her that, no, I did not have them on my person, but I could produce them.

She then replied, "No orders, no wings."

Obviously I just laughed and shrugged it off, and I returned later that day with my orders to clear up the matter, but you can see here is a perfect example of how keeping an "I-love-me book" can save you. Had I not been able to produce those orders right then and there, it would have been a "nut roll" trying to go through the process of digging all that up just to have it added to my ORB.

Side note: I subsequently found out, after looking at my new issue ORB, that, according to it, I had never served in Iraq, never went to an NCO development course, was not air-assault qualified, and was a 92Y (supply personnel) when I was enlisted (WTF!).

This all goes to show you how important it is to maintain your records and keep them current. You don't want to be that guy running around like a chicken with his head cut off during out-processing because half his deployments are missing off his DD-214 and he can't track down his orders.

Proper References

On your way out, it's always a good idea to approach your immediate supervisor and ask if he or she will write you a recommendation. This can be a general recommendation or a recommendation specific to a particular school. Regardless, leaving with not even so much as a general recommendation may prove troublesome once you're out and realize you need recommendations and can no longer track down any of your immediate supervisors or the simple sense of urgency is no longer there because you aren't face to face with them anymore. Or maybe enough time has gone by that he or she cannot give a properly accurate assessment of your performance or accomplishments and the last thing you want is a cookie cutter "he was awesome" recommendation—colleges see right through that.

This applies to everyone, from young enlisted ending their terms of service to pursue their two- or four-year degrees to senior officers pursuing their doctorates. Make sure you sit that leader down and have him provide you with a proper honest recommendation.

It is also a good idea to get recommendations from peers, because peers can often be the most honest and scrutinizing. They also *really* know what you did and what you are capable of.

I would advise leaving with at least three different leader general recommendations and three different peer general recommendations that you can use for any school. You can also use the same individuals for specific recommendations, but having a solid portfolio of general recommendations regarding character, drive, aptitude, initiative, and accomplishment is key.

Guide to Applications

In my experience applications are generally pretty similar across the board. Although you will see differences between what an undergraduate v. graduate v. doctoral application looks like, each category will usually be streamlined within itself simply for the sake of simplicity.

A lot of colleges have actually gone to generalized online applications that can be submitted to any college. Then certain colleges may require additional supplements such as essays or writing samples. The website used by the majority of undergraduate institutions in their undergraduate admissions is now https://www.commonapp.org/, simply to streamline the process. It allows you to fill parts out and then return and fill out other parts as you piece together your necessary paperwork and credentials.

Many colleges also offer a checklist that helps you to keep track of everything that you have to submit for admission by the deadline. Sometimes the application process can be overwhelming, but just remember you were *in the military*. If an application process scares you, then you need to just go ahead and start "beatin' your face."

This is also going to be where you need that portfolio of recommendations as most institutions will require at least three, and no, none of them can be from your mommy. Most applications will require a fee, usually around twenty-five to one hundred dollars, but some of these may be waived due to your veteran status, so pay attention to that. Any time you can save money is always a bonus. More for the beer fund.

You also have an edge over your civilian peer applicants when it comes to the essay portion. An essay about a tour in Baghdad putting "boot to ass," or an essay about being on a "six-month float on the Eisenhower" is sure to hold the attention of the person reading it longer and more intensely than an essay about a summer spent as a guidance counselor at Camp Immokalee. However, understand that these essays are not just looked at for content but measure the ability of the applicant to clearly and concisely convey their message with proper grammar, form, and verbiage.

Chapter 2

Americans with Disabilities Act; Accommodations and Seeking Treatment; Dealing with Physical Disabilities and Mental Health Issues in the Academic Environment

IN THIS SECTION WE'LL go over several of the programs and resources that are available to you as well as the entitlements (as much as I hate to use this word, although I think appropriate in regards to veterans' programs) that you have earned.

I didn't know a lot of these things when I transitioned and found out along the way about the differences between certain programs and the pros and cons of each. I also learned quite a bit about the Americans with Disabilities Act that, like myself, many of you will refuse to believe or acknowledge that it applies to and can benefit your situation.

I also go over a little about what it's like to deal with disabilities in the academic environment, both physically and mentally, and the importance of making sure you stay on top of your issues before other people make them their issues and use them as a tool to be a pain in your ass while you try to achieve your goals.

ADA Overview

Now I'm not here to give you a word by word boring-ass statutory regurgitation of the Americans with Disabilities Act, but suffice it to say that the majority of veterans probably have a qualifying disability that is covered by this law. Basically what the ADA says is that anyone with a disability should be able to participate in daily life the same way that someone without a disability does in regards to our purpose, education and employment. This in a sense creates a "level playing field" (another term I hate, but when it comes to veterans, I say we deserve every leg up we can get).

The way the ADA creates a level playing field in the academic environment for those with disabilities is by providing "accommodations" for those individuals by installing ramps and elevators for those with wheelchairs, resources for the deaf and blind, etc. It also creates accommodations for those with mental health issues.

This was something I had no idea about when I went back to school, and I was actually kind of sickened by it at the time in some regard, because I felt like there were a lot of students who were getting over because they could afford to pay some doctor to diagnose them with ADHD so they would be afforded more time on tests. Yup, you heard it right: if you are diagnosed with a mental disorder governed under the ADA, you can request *more time on your tests*!

Now to me, and most of you, this is appalling. How can you graduate and honestly look yourself in the mirror thinking you accomplished the same thing everyone else did when you had extra time to do it? I actually was very outspoken against accommodations my first year of law school and found myself in the dean's office after asking my professor in the middle of class (one largely full of the aforementioned trust fund babies "diagnosed" with ADHD), "If they get extra time on tests in law school, does that mean when we're in court after we graduate they get extra time to argue their case?"

While a lot of my classmates thought it was a funny comment, those receiving the extra time (who are not formally identified to the rest of the class) did not, and I soon found myself in hot water for "bullying." Yes, even grownups apparently can be bullied. Seems oxymoronic to me, but I digress.

So after witnessing this shit show of academic "equality," I did my research and found out that those diagnosed with PTSD, TBI, anxiety, and/or depression disorders were also protected under the ADA and were entitled to "reasonable accommodations." So I said, "Fuck it. How I can I use this to my advantage?"

Now, I knew I didn't need more time on tests, and I knew I didn't have any learning disabilities. I just had an "I-wanna-kick-you-in-your-larynx-all-the-time" disability. I also had at least two mandatory VA appointments a month to continue receiving my education and disability benefits, but these caused me a problem because they were often in the middle of the day and we all know a trip to the VA is an all-day affair.

This caused me problems in that I would be in violation of the mandatory-attendance policy, causing me to fail if I were to make all my appointments. This created a catch-22 in which I had to go to my appointments to get my benefits that I needed for school, but if I missed that many classes I would be flunked out. Talk about good communication between organizations! The school that relied on the funds that were made available through my participation in the program that was subsidizing their school was gonna kick me out for fulfilling the requirements of that program. Sounds about right.

Anyway, I created a case that, under the ADA, a veteran addressing diagnosed disabilities should be afforded more allowable absences under the school attendance policy. You should've seen the reaction to that. You would have sworn I walked into the president of the university's office and took a shit on his desk. Everyone was up in arms against it and looked at me like I was crazy, all after having done everything but drop an anvil on my head when I voiced my opinion about extra time on tests for those with ADHD. Shit, if anything they were the ones receiving a benefit by getting extra time while I was going to be missing class.

But much like in all walks of like, things just didn't make any sense. While students without disabilities were free to use their absences to get drunk and go to the beach, I would be forced to use all mine up and risk exceeding them to receive treatment for my issues. While it was never officially adopted by the school as policy, I was lucky enough to have professors who were sympathetic to the cause and understood my situation. I understand that this issue is now a topic of discussion for a change in the official attendance policy. So that is nice.

Making yourself aware and keeping yourself informed of how you are protected will go a long way in getting yourself out of a pinch. Had I not researched and found out that I was covered under this law, I may very well have been railroaded at some point for missing too many classes or for one of the many outbursts I had in class where I called one of my professors an idiot or one of my fellow students an asshole. PTSD is a bitch.

Montgomery GI Bill v. Post-9/11 GI Bill

Now this subject is nothing but brass tacks. There are no cool anecdotes or funny stories, just pure information. Many of you reading this will probably only be eligible for the Post 9/11, but those of you like myself who had to choose, it's an important decision.

The website https://www.gijobs.com/difference-between-the-post-9-11-gi-bill-and-montgomery-gi-bill/ is an independent site, but it is the best for comparing the two and also has links to other sites as well as resources to help service members ending their terms of service. The following explanation is verbatim from the site:

> Montgomery GI Bill: Benefit of up to $1,648 per month for 36 months. These payments are made to the student during the time they are actively enrolled in school. The benefits will increase on Oct. 1 of each year based on increases in the average undergraduate tuition in the U.S. using data from the National Center for Education Statistics.

> Post-9/11 GI Bill: Benefits will match 100 percent tuition up to the cost of the most expensive public state schools in-state undergraduate tuition. Plus, the Yellow Ribbon Program allows the schools to waive a portion of the remainder and the VA to match that waiver and increase the benefit considerably, depending on each school's unique agreement.

Which one you choose will depend on a lot of factors: obviously, whether or not you decide to attend a public school versus a more expensive private school; and whether or not you've received the Yellow Ribbon Scholarship, which many schools use to subsidize or sometimes—but not always (especially more expensive private schools)—pay the difference.

For me, it was more beneficial to use the Montgomery GI Bill during my undergrad in which I only used my first two years of it. My undergraduate institution was relatively cheap for me because I was a resident of the state, thus making my tuition significantly cheaper than it would have been if I wasn't. So I actually made money off it in a sense, because it went straight into my pocket, whereas had I used the Post-9/11, I would have lost out on some money, and it would have gone straight to the school.

Then I was able to switch to the Post-9/11 GI Bill for law school, which benefited me more there, because I went to an extremely expensive private school. So make sure you consider all of these factors before you make the decision.

Rules on the GI Bill are constantly changing as well so make sure you keep on top of them. I've seen them change quite a bit during my time, and I was lucky I was grandfathered in on a few things that affected my choices. From the time this is published to the time you read it, things may very well have changed, so be sure to do your research.

Also keep in mind that some states offer free or reduced tuition for veterans. There are also some states that waive the residency requirement for their state-school tuition. I didn't know this, or I may very well have chosen to go somewhere else, so this should be a huge consideration when you decide whether or not to stick around post/ base, go home, or relocate for your education.

VA Benefit Blog at http://vabenefitblog.com/which-gi-bill-is-right-for-me-%E2%80%93-the-montgomery-or-post-911/ is a good blog run by a pretty knowledgeable dude on the subject, and the blog allows for you to interact by asking questions, which is nice. He also has links and blogs concerning other benefits as well.

Vet Jobs at http://vetjobs.com/the-states-that-offer-tuition-waivers-for-student-veterans/ has the most comprehensive list and explanation of benefits in regards to what particular states do for their veterans. It's also a leading job board for veterans as well, so just like a lot of the other sites I've picked out to include in this book, it provides multiple resources and tools for you to use.

The United States Department of Veterans Affairs at http://www.va.gov/ is obviously your go-to source for everything, but I find that the private sites typically break things down better and are good at weeding through all the bureaucratic bullshit we all know and love.

VA Vocational Rehab

Vocational rehabilitation is for those with service-connected disabilities. It offers some different options, especially for those not looking to go the regular four-year route. VR keys off your abilities, skills, qualifications, and realistic goals. It then examines the job market in your given area and allows you to choose a profession or sometimes even college as well. It really depends on the area.

I applied for VR in my area to see if they would pay for my law school, but the area I was in was so saturated with attorneys that they looked at me like I was nuts. Yet a buddy of mine who's a West Point grad had his MBA at Harvard paid for through VR. Go figure.

Anyway, this is definitely another consideration when deciding where you want to go and what you want to do. If you qualify you could wind up getting a full ride instead of the basics that the GI Bill provides. I've also known soldiers who have used it to attend trade schools and even had things like their tools, laptops, and gas to and from school paid for through the program.

This is probably one of the most overlooked programs by many veterans. You also maintain some eligibility after you have used your GI Bill if you are unemployed in your field and can show to your counselor (there is a mandatory screening process) that you would be more successful in a different career and that career is in need of personnel in your area.

You can apply for VR at your local VA, the big ones, though. I've never seen one at a community-based outpatient clinic (CBOC), but some areas may have them. Keep in mind, though, that you must have a service-connected disability to qualify, and it is definitely a lengthy process. It took me three months just to get an initial appointment when I got out, but it's still worth it, even if you're already attending school, because they can transfer your GI Bill over once you're approved, and it will serve your purpose in the long run.

Word of caution: *Do not miss your appointment!* If you miss your initial counseling/eligibility appointment, you aren't eligible to apply again for a year. The VA actually has a good blog site called "VAntage Point" that compares all three programs and allows you to ask questions as well at http://www.blogs.va.gov/VAntage/4237/voc-rehab-and-the-gi-bill-what%E2%80%99s-the-difference/. Once again this is one of those sites which provides multiple sources for all different types of categories, including employment and other benefits.

Dealing with Disabilities

When I went back to school, I had everything from a broken back to PTSD, TBI, hearing loss, and just general "fuck-civilians" disease. So while I didn't realize I was coming in to the academic environment with a disadvantage, I certainly was. Service members tend not to acknowledge their problems and treat any such acknowledgment as a sign of weakness. We believe that civilians do not operate on our level, and we do more from five to nine in the morning than they do from nine to five in the afternoon.

However, the operational tempo is different. Despite most people looking at the military as this extremely structured organization, it teaches its members to be able to fly by the seat of their pants and to be versatile. Our mind-sets are tuned differently to manage and prioritize our time based on importance of issue.

I once had a professor in undergrad ask me, "Why are you always late? Aren't you in the army? Aren't you guys always on time?"

To that I replied by laughing and saying, "When it's a matter of importance," to which he did not respond kindly. I've seen some law students cry because they were running late. You get the idea.

Although this doesn't necessarily speak to the issue of disability per se, it speaks to how our minds have been tuned. In a sense, experiencing PTSD and TBI is much the same, a tuning of our minds. From the stupid questions I will address later to what I previously stated in terms of just "not givin' a shit," these issues are also exacerbated by the fact that you are no longer surrounded by a group of individuals who are basically experiencing the same issues. I know that in the unit I was in prior to going back to school, every single individual was diagnosed with PTSD and many with TBI and physical issues. But being that we all were dealing with the same issues, it created an environment in which it was as if that issue simply didn't exist.

It's the opposite when you get to school where most of your colleagues still believe in Santa Claus and the Easter bunny. Acknowledging this is the first step to dealing with the issue. By understanding that this is not a weakness but just something you're going to ultimately have to control, you can see to it that it doesn't become a problem for you.

You are going to do or say something that offends someone at some point. It's almost impossible not to, even if it's just a reaction to someone else's comment that you yourself might deem inappropriate. You have to remember that you are outnumbered in this environment, and people probably already have a preconceived notion or stereotype of you, regardless of what it may be.

If you have been diagnosed with PTSD, you need to understand the symptoms so you can mitigate any reactions these may cause if you get into a situation that triggers them. Once you recognize and get a handle on it, then you can begin to identify and stay away from situations that may cause a negative outcome and maybe even learn to use it to your advantage.

As to dealing with physical disabilities, my only real experience was sitting in uncomfortable chairs, so my only real advice there is to make sure you always have some ibuprofen with you.

Continuing Treatment while in School

Many times while in school we neglect our health. With the time restraints on us from class to studying to our personal obligations, it seems to be the first thing out the window. This is totally backward. How are you going to complete the mission if you are sick or injured?

Despite our "combat" mind-set we do not need to "suck it up and drive on," when we're not feeling well like we're about to take a machine gun nest in order to win a decisive battle. Take care of yourself. If you are sick or injured, seek treatment so it doesn't snowball into something that will ultimately really take you out of the fight. Every school has a clinic, and most large universities, a hospital. This will most likely be provided to you free of charge through your student health insurance, but rely on your VA assets as well.

You will undoubtedly catch something from one of the more "scum-baggier" students who still haven't managed to learn how to do laundry or wipe their own asses yet. Many times this happens around midterms. It's usually approaching season change, stress levels are high, and immune systems are lowered. So make sure to take care of your health.

The last semester of law school, I broke my leg. I got run over by a taxi cab in the parking lot of a strip club. True story. Anyway, I went from a hard cast and crutches to a soft cast and crutches to a "Japanese jump boot" over the course of four months. I couldn't drive. I was working in a legal clinic as an intern (the veterans' clinic, ironically enough), so I was in a friggin' suit with a briefcase every day. Try carrying a heavy-ass briefcase one hundred meters while you're on crutches—fun times. It was also on the second floor of the law school and the elevator sucked, so I had to hop up the stairs every day. And I had to be at court a lot. I also had a desk that weighed about a hundred pounds break and fall apart on top of me that semester, so needless to say, that semester physically *sucked*! I don't know if karma was catching up with me for something I did or what, but I dealt with it.

The point is that I made sure to go to my appointments and get the treatment I needed so as not to neglect my healing process and still maintain what I needed to in order to be successful. I can't tell you how many times colleagues of mine came up and told me they thought I was nuts and that they would have taken the semester off. This just goes to show you, once again, the mind-set that we have that is often absent in civilians that gives you a leg up on the scholarly battlefield.

I also must acknowledge as well that, had I not had a good support base in my local veteran friends, I wouldn't have been able to finish that semester. Without the help of my good friend Alec, I wouldn't have been able to get to school or do a lot of the things I needed to do to handle business.

With that being said, you also have to consider your existing health issues and continue treatment. Letting things fall by the wayside that have already been diagnosed is not the answer either. If you have VA benefits or a pension, make sure you establish a primary care physician that you like, not one that just goes through the motions. I know I went through at least three before I found a really good one.

Also, if you have specialists, physical therapy, or mental health professionals you should be seeing, maintain that as well. I know that the VA near me recently opened up physical therapy and other specialty clinics for night and weekend hours specifically due to the large influx of students needing these services in the region that are unable to make these appointments during the day. Do not forgo your health for the sake of an expensive piece of paper. The primary objective of this book is to get you that diploma, but you can't do it if you are not physically and mentally healthy.

Chapter 3

Recon the Objective

Just like anything in the military, we are taught to recon the objective. You don't walk straight into an ambush if you can help it. You make a plan, send out a team, gather intelligence, and report back. That information is used to develop the ultimate plan, the plan that will become the mission.

Finding the Right School for You

I cannot stress enough how important this is, and I can say from a personal standpoint that I have made mistakes in this area. Although I ultimately graduated basically where I grew up, I did have other colleges I was interested in right out of high school. I was a high school athlete, and one of my priorities as a young eighteen-year-old idiot was to pick the school where I knew I could start and had an awesome party scene.

Now don't get me wrong the social environment of a school is very important, but you need to establish clear priorities. My choices as an incoming freshman were Penn State, University of Pittsburgh, and Western Maryland College (McDaniel College now). I made sure to visit each campus, and I had a great time at each one. And each one brought something unique to the table. I loved the city, so University of Pittsburgh was a great choice. Penn State was Penn State.

But when I showed up for my recruiting trip to Western Maryland, they showed me the time of my life. It was a small campus, and it was a great academic institution in the same conference as William and Mary, Johns Hopkins, Moravian, and Muhlenberg. And I knew that I could be a big fish in a little pond there, rather than a small fish in a big pond at one of the other institutions. I knew that the wrestling team had a spot for me, and after my visit there, my decision was made.

After a year I burnt myself out—academically, athletically, socially. I had basically used up all of the resources that school had to offer me in one year. So I made the decision to transfer. This time, the decision was between Lehigh University and Temple University. I made the decision to go home and attend one of the largest and most diverse schools in the country, and I couldn't have been happier with my choice. I chose Temple, and although I had to make the decision to end my college athletic career much earlier than I expected, it was a better fit for me.

Temple wasn't even on my initial radar coming out of high school, because to me, it was too close to home. Yet the resources that Temple offered me allowed me to excel in every aspect of my education. Had I done a proper initial recon with a checklist with proper priorities, I would have been able to avoid this process. This is not to say I didn't enjoy my first-year experience, and students do often transfer, many times immediately after their freshman year. The difference here, between you and me, is I was a naïve eighteen-year-old idiot straight out of high school really just seeking independence as priority one, which I believe quite frankly is the objective of most college freshman.

It isn't typically till our junior years that we really settle in and realize that the outcome after these four years dictates much of where we will be directed in our futures. But you have an advantage here. You are socially beyond your peers and have experienced things that have propelled you into a different social stratum, one that has made you more mature, disciplined, and wise.

You have the ability that the eighteen-year-old frosh doesn't have to make calculated well-reasoned decisions based on need, practicality, and priority. You are able to sit down and make a list of what it is that you truly need to make your life better and to put you in a position to pursue your goals in the civilian world.

Many of you have families now. Many of you have lived in different states, different countries, have deployed to combat zones, and have access to a part of your brain that the initial college entrant does not. Use that to your advantage to make the right decision based on need, practicality, and priority.

Make Visits a Priority

Once again, this needs to be a priority. I chose one of my schools sight unseen because I was in a rush to meet the application deadline and I was six months from discharge and just pulled the trigger based on its geographical location and a decent website. Bad idea.

Make sure you physically go to the school. Check out the buildings, the surrounding areas, the restaurants, the demographics, the schools for your children, *everything*. Believe me: you will regret it if you decide to go to a school just because it's near the beach and has a cool shark as its mascot. If you can't make time or can't afford to visit then maybe that's not the school for you.

Now don't get all "sad sally" because I'm telling you something you don't want to hear, but if you're from Jersey and you want to go to UCLA but can't afford to visit the school, you might not like what you got yourself into. This is where you make your school wish list.

You have your "reach" school, or the school that you really want to go to but are not sure if you can get in. You have your "maybe" schools you like and are pretty sure that you can get into. Then you have your "safety" schools you know you can definitely get into.

Now your safeties should obviously be schools you like too, but at the end of the day, you don't want to be stuck with five applications and five denials, because the ultimate goal here is to further your education in order to make you more marketable in the civilian world. Remember the story of the eighteen-year-old me? Jacked-up priorities led to me bouncing from school to school.

Once you have your list of schools, you prioritize your visits based on your priority list. We will get to this later. Once you have visited each school, you make a pro/con list for each one. What did you love, what did you like, what did you not like, and what did you hate? You will be amazed at how functional, practical and helpful this will be to you in making your ultimate decision. Once you have made these lists be realistic and stack them in order and reassess which school you really want to attend.

Consider Not Only the Academic Environment but the Social Scene and Family Orientation

Many of you will be getting out after your first tour and will still be in your early twenties. You may feel like you missed out on the college experience that many of your friends experienced while you were off "fighting the good fight." Do not let this distract you from making the right decision when it comes to what school you want to attend.

With that being said college is as much a social education as it is academic. You learn how to properly interact with others and how to develop friendly and romantic relationships, and you grow out of your immature, dependent self into a mature, independent self—hopefully.

On your visits, take notice of the social scene on campus. What are your interests? You're not just a number, rank, or uniform here. You have particular hobbies, sports you engage in, instruments you play. Take the time to notice the atmosphere of the campus and see whether or not it will not only facilitate your academic progress but advance your personal and social interests as well.

I know that when I went to Temple, my head was spinning just reading the newsletter about the events, clubs, sports, and shows, everything that was going on. There was a club for everyone, and if there wasn't, all it took was three people to start one—it was amazing.

You will find that some campuses are more rigid than others; maybe that's what you are looking for or still need during your transition. I know it took me time to ease back into the culture that is Philadelphia and; specifically; Temple University after six years in the army stationed in the South. But it's important for your growth. It's important for your family, and it's important for your success. You don't want to be the veteran in the back of the class still wearing a high and tight and desert boots. Believe me: I've run into them, and they're just holding on too tight. You're starting a new chapter in your life and need to adjust as such.

Now I don't recommend growing your hair down to your ass, stopping taking showers, and becoming a hippie either, but you get the idea. You will learn to once again interact with the civilian population in ways that don't involve calling them the F word and shooting knife hands at their faces all the time.

Once again, this is an area I wish I had more guidance in, because I had a hard time with my reintegration into the student population. I recently saw a meme on a veteran website that made me laugh out loud. At the top it read, "What it feels like," and at the bottom, "Using my GI Bill" and the picture was of Billy Madison sitting in a kindergarten class room. You will feel like that. Even if some of the students are your own age or a couple years younger, your life experience has aged you beyond the number on your birthday cake.

Still others of you will be going back to college after five, ten, fifteen, twenty years of service, and you will truly be steaming out of your ears. So assess the environment. Maybe night school is best for you where the crowd is a little more mature and experienced in life. Consider that you will learn more from them than from younger peers, but do not discount some of the gems of wisdom that tend to drop out of the mouths of some of the younger students.

Those of you with families will have yet another consideration. Are there good schools for my children near the institution? Are there good jobs for my wife or husband? All of these are considerations and will land at the top of your priority list when making your decision in choosing your school.

Priorities

Finally, priorities. I know that I have spoken about this throughout the chapter, but I have left it last because I want to reiterate its importance. I'd also like to provide you with a sample checklist much like the one I would put together now had I had someone giving me the advice I'm imparting on you.

Priority lists are going to be different for everyone, but there will be four main areas that will be on *everyone's* list, and if they are not, go ahead and assume the front leaning rest. Now these will not be in the same order for everyone, but *family, location, cost,* and *programs* will or at least should be on everyone's priority list at the top. In whichever order yours fall makes no difference as long as these four are at the top.

Now you will have supplemental priorities such as social setting, favorite football team, etc. But even these subsets ultimately fit into these four top priorities. Here's an example of what mine would have looked like had I the forethought to make one:

> **Location**: I knew when I got out that I ultimately wanted to settle back home, so my priority schools should be in that area.
>
> **Cost**: I knew that I only had a year left on my GI Bill, so I have to make sure that I attend a school that I cannot only afford once my GI Bill runs out, but I also have to take into consideration the cost of living and ability to receive financial aid while I'm in school and unable to work. How much is it going to cost to relocate?
>
> **Programs**: I know that the program I'm going into is general so it doesn't really matter where I go it's all going to be the same information

Family: Family is kind of a moot point here because I'm not married. And in terms of being close to my immediate family, that ties in to location, so once again, moot point

Social Scene: Are there likeminded people here? Am I going to thrive in this environment or just survive?

Night Life: As a single guy, is there a vibrant social culture conducive to meeting new people, and if not, I'll be home anyway, so I'll know people.

Weather: Hot or cold?

You can begin to see how a lot of these will start to intertwine or even become subsets of the "big four" (weather as a subset of location), and you can really get a sense after you've compiled your schools which one floats to the top. Now a priority list for a recent retiree with a family of four might look something more like this:

Family: We have been stationed here for five years, and I don't want to uproot my family.

Location: I have to stay pretty close to the area because of my family.

Cost: I deferred my GI Bill to my wife, so I have to pay out of pocket.

Programs: I'd really like to study aerospace engineering.

Hunting: My favorite hobby is hunting, and this is some of the best hunting around.

The single social scene and other subjects would not even land on this individual's list (I would hope not), but he has other subsets.

You can see how everyone's priority list is different. A lot of SMs do decide to settle right outside their last duty station, and luckily there are a lot of good schools around our posts and bases.

Still yet, a large number of SMs, even those with families, decide to return back to their original home or even start fresh somewhere new. These are all considerations that tie into your ultimate decision. Sometimes you don't end up with your dream school, but you end up with the school that's best for you.

Chapter 4

Initiate a Plan and Establish a Schedule

Now you've made your priority list, you've visited your schools, you've applied, and you've been accepted. You're in. You've seized the objective, and now it's on to mission two: completing your education.

Just like any military operation and just like the previous portion, gaining admission, it is important to have a plan. Murphy's Law dictates that anything that can go wrong will go wrong, but at least with a plan we can fight him a little bit.

As prior military, you have acquired a set of skills—skills that make you dangerous to guys like Murphy. The most important of these skills in regards to completing your academic endeavors is discipline. Throughout our careers we have been exposed to numerous OPORDERS, FRAGOS, and task-to-do lists, risk assessments, WARNOS, and every other acronym on the planet that just means *plan*. So why would we not make a plan for the next step of our lives and an extremely important one at that, completing our civilian education?

Although in theory this is the easiest part of the process, it will be the hardest part to actually stick to. Once again I'm reminded of a meme I recently saw on the same veterans' website. It was a picture of a young veteran on the phone shouting, "I fuckin' been to war! Eight-thirty class ain't shit!" The next picture is of the veteran still sleeping with beer bottles all over the floor and the alarm clock blinking 0930. I have definitely been there. I hate to say it, but this has been much the nature of our veteran generation. PTSD, TBI, uneasy assimilation, simple lack of interest, and a whole host of other factors contribute to it. I hate to blame the media, but in some circumstances, these problems have become self-fulfilling prophecies because of the overpromotion of so-called veterans-help organizations that just make us look like wounded animals unable to manage our problems and health issues. Once again I speak from experience here, and I'm telling you that had I made a plan and really stuck to it, the same thing probably wouldn't have happened to me—more than once.

Using Your Military Discipline to Plan, Execute, and Achieve

Remember that first day of basic or boot when you had no fucking idea what was going on? Let's go ahead and see to it that that does not happen on your first day of class. Because just like basic and boot, you will be excited, nervous, anxious, and scared shitless—not because you're going into some major engagement or things are about to suck, but because it's *new*.

And if it's not necessarily new but you're simply going back, it will be different. Campus will be bustling with all types of distractions. Your first class will be on one side of the campus, and your next will be on the completely opposite side in the *back forty*. Then all of a sudden FRAGO! Your classroom has changed to another classroom. The first day is nothing but a series of "fuck-fuck games" just like basic or boot, but you're used to it. So don't let the fact that you're in a different environment dictate your plan, just adapt and overcome.

Use the same skills you used in the military to overcome obstacles and unexpected hurdles. Do your proper recon of the campus before your first day. Map out your route and make an alternate route in case that one becomes compromised. I know this may sound corny to you now, but you will thank me that you did. It's a huge stress reducer, and once you settle into your schedule and ease into the semester, you'll become more at ease just like you became week three/week four of training. Utilizing your skills to do this will not only make things easier on you, but it will reduce stress, which will reduce anxiety, which will reduce the chance that you will have any issues.

Do this not only with your classes but with everything in your academic life in order to relieve yourself of stress and ensure that you achieve your goals through proper planning. The first day you are late for a class, it won't be the professor or the other students that look down on you or quite frankly even care half the time—it'll be you, because you know that you should be held to a higher standard, and if you're not early, you're late.

Now that we have the timing and routes mapped and alleviated ourselves of that problem, we turn our attention to actual class. If you come to class unprepared, you might as well not come at all. Not only will you be stressed because you forgot your pen, now you have to ask someone else for one, and they think you're a football bat, and now the professor is looking at you.

Make a packing list. We did it for a leisurely five-mile road march. Why would we not do it for something as important as class? As we progress through the plan, execute, achieve phase, you can see how everything that we're doing to prepare for the end state, which is graduation, is nothing more than we did to prepare for the end state of any mission we've ever been tasked with.

Maintaining a Schedule Conducive to Your Expectations

Once you've established your schedule and you've gone to your first few classes, you'll come to understand what it is your professors expect of you, and you will certainly have expectations of them. And believe it or not, your classmates will have expectations of you too. Live up to them. You still represent the military. You always will. That pride will never die inside of you, and you should be proud of that, so transfer that into the work that you do on the scholarly battlefield.

With that being said, if you realize that you can no longer sustain a certain schedule, drop a class. Or if you realize you can take on more, add a class. But the important thing to remember is to tailor your schedule conducive to your expectations and abilities. There's no shame if everyone else is taking twelve credits and you're taking ten that semester. *Do you.*

Don't let someone—a parent, a spouse, a peer—push you into too much. I have made this mistake time and time again, letting someone else dictate my path. In the end, it's about your happiness and expectations, not anyone else's.

You're not going to give the mod deuce to someone who can't carry it when you know they'll fail even though they will likely try their hardest to succeed. It's just not practical. So it's not fair to yourself to put yourself in a situation where you will not just survive but thrive. If taking an extra two semesters to graduate when all your buddies are graduating now means the difference between a 2.5 and a 3.0, *do it.*

This goes the other way too, if you realize that classes are a breeze and you can graduate early, *do it.* It will save you money and time and put you out in front of your peers when it comes to the job market.

It's also important to pick a major and take classes that you like. Hell, I changed my major three or four times. But in the end, I was happy, not miserable like a lot of my colleagues who stuck out their original majors just because they thought it would get them a job and then wound up doing something completely different anyway. Pick something that you're passionate about, because then you will excel at it. If you pick something simply out of practicality, you might wind up having a miserable educational experience.

Now don't get me wrong. Don't go to college for underwater basket weaving just because you like to make baskets while scuba diving, but make sure you pick something you know you will see through because you want to see through. In the end it will pay dividends.

Then remember that you need to leave yourself time for extracurricular and social interaction otherwise you will go nuts. Maintain a schedule conducive to your expectations.

The Importance of Being Regimented

Without being regimented, the military would not operate properly. Without being regimented, the civilian world would not operate properly either. This goes for academic life as well. Although spontaneity can be great at times, it doesn't have much room in the academic environment where you literally have a schedule governed by a clock and bells. Nothing more needs to be said about this than to just remember to always be on time.

Chapter 5

Create a Foundation of Support

Just like any military mission, it is always important to establish a base or foundation of support, someone or something you can rely on in case shit hits the fan on the objective. In the academic environment, this can be professors, family, friends, sports organizations, etc. Just having someone there to let you know that you're on the right azimuth and that you're "trackin'" is enough sometimes just to get you through a rough patch. Without this, your experience will be miserable and may ultimately end in a failed mission

Friends and Family

Surround yourself with people of high quality, people with the same goals, and people who will help you achieve yours. Those of you who enter this academic endeavor with a family will undoubtedly have a different type of experience than those who don't. My nearest family member was over a thousand miles away. I went through my last academic experience knowing absolutely no one when I got there, but my time in the military and changing posts several times over almost ten years prepared me for that.

This goes back to your priority list. Had I made a proper priority list, I would have known that location should have been priority one in order to land me back where I wanted to be. Most single SMs will wind up back where they are originally from, so they will have the support of their immediate family and friends, and in my experience most married SMs usually settle around their last duty station, so they not only have the support of their families, but also those of their comrades in arms still stationed nearby.

However, there are times where relationships with your family or friends can be toxic—*cut them off,* at least for the time while you're in school trying to complete your goal of graduation. Negative support is not good, and nobody is better at meddling in your affairs than those closest to you.

Remember that you need to set your own goals conducive to your expectations, or you will be miserable and may ultimately fail. If your parents want you to be a lawyer or a doctor and you really want to be a mechanic, be a mechanic. Money and prestige and titles aren't everything—happiness is.

I have a buddy with a psychology degree from Lehigh who pulls motors apart for a living and is covered in grease all day. The guy is happy working on and riding dirt bikes every day. My brother has an honors degree from Temple in biological anthropology, was a medical officer, and he chops trees down, plays poker, and hunts deer all day. I wish we were all so lucky.

I spent three years in law school and owe a fortune in student loans just to learn how broken the legal system really is and that the general perception of lawyers is correct—they really are overpaid, self-absorbed assholes.

I should've became a tattoo artist when I got out. So don't let anyone dictate your path. Like I said before, you may change your major several times before you find out what it is you are really interested in, but don't be afraid to make that change.

Medical and Mental Health

How you leave the service will decide on how you approach this animal. If you retire, you will likely retain your Tricare insurance. If you simply ETS, you are going to want to look at your options before you hit the ground running. The website http://www.vetsfirst.org/ military-separation-guide/ is a great site for SMs about to end their term of service.

Most colleges and universities offer student health insurance plans, and some even make them mandatory and include them in your tuition, so make sure to look into that because either way you're going to want to be covered.

Remember basic and boot when everyone got hit with the "Joe Crud Bug" or basically a cold or flu. Anything like that flourishes just as well in the dorms or suites if you choose to live on campus among your scholarly colleagues. If you're leaving with any type of disability, make sure to establish where the closest VA is as well, as they can often alleviate healthcare costs for vets and sometimes provide free services like flu shots.

Make sure you take care of all of this before starting school, because the last thing you want to worry about is trying to square away your health insurance while you're sick in school studying for midterms, which—don't ask me why—seems to be the time everyone gets sick.

Mental health is of the utmost importance as well. Many of us are leaving the service with PTSD, TBI, depression, and anxiety disorders.

Do not let these go untreated!

Do not try to be the tough guy or girl and think you can just get through it without proper treatment. It will bottle up and bottle up and eventually become an issue. You'll wind up beating one of your classmates with your textbook one day just for brushing you in the hallway.

You have to remember that despite the fact you may be getting by with these issues while you're still in the service, you're surrounded by people with the same issues. Once you leave the military, you will be inserted into an environment where not only do the majority of your colleagues not have these issues, but also they don't understand them.

These conditions can often be misinterpreted not only by students but professors and administrators, which can cause you significant disciplinary or other issues if something happens. See someone. Most campuses offer counselors and mental health advisors you can utilize. We all know by now that it's not a sign of weakness, so don't think that you're in the civilian world you have to hide it by not continuing treatment.

I can't stress this enough. Do what you need to do to keep your head in the game, and if you are prescribed medications, *take them*. If you believe that the medications you're being prescribed aren't working or are making the problem worse, then *speak up*. Let your doctor know. Go to the VA. Do what you got to do to make sure that your mental health does not stand in the way of your success.

Veteran Groups and Organizations

Join the VFW. If not just for a sense of belonging and cheap beer, do it because they advocate for our rights on Capitol Hill. It will give you a sense of pride once you get out to know that you belong to such a prestigious organization.

Join the American Legion. Do something that keeps you engaged in the veteran community so that you're always reminded that you are different. These places also provide solace in case you would rather talk to a brother or sister than a school mental health counselor.

Join your school's veterans' organization. Many are popping up as many of us are leaving the service and dropping into college campuses all over the United States. If your school doesn't have one, start one. I guarantee that, once you do, brothers and sisters will come out of the woodwork. Sometimes it just takes that one person to be bold. These groups help to keep us unified and give us an outlet as well as social circle to interact in. They can often double as study groups as you come to find that many SMs tend to migrate toward majors in criminal justice and the political sciences.

Keeping Contact with Brothers and Sisters from Service

Do not lose contact with those you served with. Oftentimes we form bonds with them closer than those we have with our own blood. I love getting random phone calls or Facebook messages or e-mails from my brothers. It fundamentally changes my day when I see a buddy having his first child or getting promoted through social media.

The fact that our generation has this capability to keep in such close contact means we should not be losing twenty-two of us a fucking day to suicide. *It is simply fucking unacceptable!* Reach out from time to time just to check up on your buddies. One phone call can change the outcome of a day. It will help you as well to stay glued to the fabric. Although you may be gung ho about getting out now, you will miss it, you will miss your units, you will miss your buddies, and it's important that you stay in contact.

Chapter 6

Reassimilation into the Civilian World and the Academic Environment

Anytime the military moves into a new area to conduct any kind of operation, be it combat or peacetime, there is an initial assimilation period. Remember that month spent in Kuwait or Saudi before deployment into Iraq or Afghanistan? Or the month spent preparing for a float? This is necessary to get the mind and the body in sync (no pun intended) with the new environment so that you can operate with maximum effect. Without this period, being plunged into a new environment can often cause several problems both physical and mental.

Before joining the military, we were all part of the civilian world so instead of having to assimilate we simply have to reassimilate. We still know the cultural norms, what to do, and what not to do. We still understand what acceptable behavior is and what isn't. But sometimes this transition can be tough. Sometimes we even fight it.

I know this was my initial problem. We are so entrenched in our military values and subcultural thinking that we forget that we have to conduct ourselves in a different manner when we enter back into the "real world."

Leaping into an Unfamiliar Environment

Although we are still familiar with the civilian environment from whence we came before joining the service, the college and university environment is a microcosm. It is an environment within an environment that expects even more from us than regular civilian life—more rules, more regulations, more adverse reaction if and when we jack something up. This is why *we thrive* on college campuses.

We already know what it's like to be in an environment within an environment—an environment that holds us to a higher standard with more rules, regulations, and harsher punishment for failure.

My first day of law school, my faculty advisor specifically sought me out and asked me if I had time to come back with him to his office to chat. I did so. I went, and as soon as I sat down, he said, "I understand you were in the military."

I told him I just got out and this was where I ended up.

He looked me dead in the eye and told me, "A lot of times guys like you will trip out the gate until you realize the same keys to success that made you succeed in the military are the same keys to success that will allow you to succeed here."

He then went on to tell me that some of the best students at the three different institutions at which he had taught as well as been a dean were prior military.

We have the initial assumption that since this isn't the military, we have to readjust our outlook on how to achieve. Although slight deviations have to be made, ultimately the same discipline and attention to detail that made you successful in the military will make you successful in the academic environment.

So although this is an unfamiliar environment, it is no different than every other unfamiliar environment we've encountered before. You do not need to be intimidated by it. Embrace the suck and just "throw your knees into the breeze."

Interaction with Professors

You will come to find that there are several different types of professors. You'll have your arrogant "I'm-tenured-so-fuck-you!" professors. You'll have your "hippies," "anarchists," "bleeding heart liberals," "socialists." You name it, its academia. You run the gamut of intellectual thought.

But you will find professors you can relate to, whether it's on a political issue or simply on a personal level. It's important to establish good relationships with your professors. Although you will certainly butt heads with a lot of them, it is important to remember they are professors because they worked hard to get there (at least in most cases), and they should be shown proper respect.

Remember that NCO or officer you hated and was always ate up? You knew that despite the fact he or she was a "soup sammich," you had to at least show respect to the rank he or she was wearing, as much as you may have hated it. I know I did. Same goes for professors.

This doesn't mean you have to agree with them. That's the point of academia—open, honest debate. Question those professors you don't agree with and provide valid points why you think your perspective might be the correct one. If they are good professors, they may still not agree with you, but they should acknowledge your points, and they will learn to respect you too.

Don't make enemies with professors. Trust me on this one. It will bite you in the ass down the road. Also make sure that you create at least a few allies in your professors. Pick their brains.

Does this sound familiar? You wouldn't want to make enemies with any of your drill sergeants or drill instructors would you? And wouldn't you want them to share their knowledge with you?

I was lucky enough in each of my academic endeavors to have at least one professor show interest in me and take me under his or her wing, in many cases saving my academic career, because unlike the advice I'm giving you here, I followed a different school of thought at the time, one of "no fucks given." I thought all my professors were assholes. I fought with them in class. I didn't have the knowledge

I have now in regards to proper academic etiquette, and I was still having problems assimilating into the academic environment.

I was thrown back into undergrad as a sergeant, green to gold selectee, almost immediately after returning from a tour in Baghdad, so I'm sure you can imagine what that was like. I was still running around with my hair on fire on one of the most liberal college campuses in the world, giving everyone a hefty middle finger everywhere I went. It took one of my professors to ask me to stay after class one day following a lecture on US Cold War foreign policy to change that.

I don't know if I was hungover or just still drunk from the night before, but he grabbed me on my way out the door. He sat me down and asked me if I was all right and told me he had seen this before. I looked at him sidewise, not knowing what he meant, and he began to tell me a story about his time in the service during the Cold War and his best friend who was a helicopter pilot in Vietnam.

He said, "You have the same look in your eye he did when he got back." Ironically enough, this really opened my eyes and made me realize that I needed to get a handle on myself. Although to other students I probably just looked like every other college kid who had a late night of partying, he was able to identify that it was something else with me, and he reached out a helping hand.

I came to know this man to be one of the most brilliant people I have ever met, and he changed the course of my education. I can honestly say that had it not been for him I may not have straightened up and done what I needed to do in undergrad. Quite frankly, I almost failed out on purpose just to meet back up with my unit in Afghanistan. He is still a mentor to me this day, and I consider him a friend.

The same thing happened to me in law school, except this professor really surprised me. We had competing political and social views, our demographics couldn't have been more opposite, and it was an unlikely match in my eyes.

But she approached me after finding out I was in the army and asked for my help on a law article she was writing about PTSD and another on the ban on women in combat arms. I happily helped her, basically with technical jargon for her article and from there sprang a relationship that was integral to my success in law school. She was my advocate every time I fell down, and I fell down a lot. She proactively looked into my wellbeing during my time there and saw to it that my experience was not as negative as it may have been without her guidance. She was also able to recognize my "thousand-yard stare" and was compassionate and accommodating when I had a death in the family and lost a few of my comrades in the box and was unable to attend funerals because of "mandatory attendance policies." She is another that I consider a mentor and a friend still today.

You will need these professors to understand these issues, because this will happen to you while you are in school, and these relationships will follow you after your academic careers as well when it comes to networking, recommendations, and job contacts. So I can't stress enough how important it is to cultivate these relationships and open yourself up to them even though sometimes you feel like you still want to remain closed off from any type of individual help or interaction from your professors or anyone else for that matter.

Interaction with Fellow Students

Your interactions with your fellow students will vary depending on where you inject yourself in the social hierarchy, whether you join some sort of social groups, and quite frankly where you go to school.

My interaction with my colleagues at Temple was quite the opposite of my interaction with my colleagues at NSU. They were just two different demographics, one that I fit into and one that I didn't. This is a subsection priority when you make your decision where to go to school, which will likely fall under location. You have to understand the backgrounds of the students you'll be in class with and adjust accordingly.

However, despite where you choose to go, the fact of the matter is that you will have to interact with your fellow students. You can try and play the recluse, back-of-the-classroom-guy game like I did for a while, but that won't last long. We're military people. We're *alphas*. We can only last so long before we have to respond to a "colleague's" stupid statement, question, comment, or assumption in class.

This is where another one of our important military skills comes into play—*tact*. You have to have tact when dealing with your fellow classmates, not just because its "classy," but also because these are the people that you are going to be sitting beside for up to the next four years and ultimately be joining and competing against in the job market.

One of the first things they tell you at orientation is "be nice to your fellow classmates, because they are the ones you will be working with, for, and against when you get outta here." This doesn't just go for law school; it goes for any institution of higher learning. If you develop nothing but negative relationships with your fellow classmates, no one is going to want to work with or for you, let alone hire you. So make sure you treat your fellow students with respect even though sometimes you may want to throat punch them.

Understanding and Tolerating Different Viewpoints

Like I spoke about before with different professor viewpoints, this applies across the board. Different students, different organizations, different janitors—they all have different viewpoints. You don't have to agree, you don't even have to understand (half the time you won't), but you do have to tolerate them to a point.

Now I'm not telling you to tolerate the viewpoints of the "let's-kick-a-baby" club, but you get what I mean. There will be organizations, students, and professors with viewpoints that will not only irk you but will downright enrage you, especially as a veteran, and they will target you and do it on purpose sometimes.

You will tend to see these more on the larger college campuses where there is a larger student population and wider range of ideals. I remember my first year of undergrad, walking across campus and seeing an antiabortion protest that was one of the most disgusting displays I have ever seen in my life, with inappropriate signs and messages that were what I can only imagine designed to psychologically damage women who have had to make that tough decision. Even prolifers were disgusted with the display, and although I wanted to wrap one of those signs around one of the protestor's necks, I had to drive on and tolerate it.

Several years later, I was in Baghdad and received a letter from my brother. He made the decision while I was overseas to join ROTC to also serve in the army, and in the letter he explained his disgust with an on-campus rally protesting the war in Iraq and demanding that all ROTC programs be removed from college campuses. While reading the letter a picture fell out onto the floor, and I picked it up. In the picture was a young student on the steps of the Temple library holding a sign saying, "No ROTC on campus," and standing one step above directly behind him was my brother holding a sign with an arrow pointing down at the student which said, "We fight for your right to do this." I lost it. I thought how genius and what an effective way to tolerate but still let your opinion be known as well.

My brother had the forethought, much unlike myself, to go about it in a respectful, witty, and tactful manner and "one up" the guy rather than respond in a way that may have well gotten him into trouble. I think that whereas I probably would have karate chopped the kid in the throat, it's almost more gratifying to win the way my brother did.

Dealing with the "Stupid Questions" You Will Inevitably Be Asked

I knew when I came back from combat, I would inevitably be asked stupid questions, number one ultimately being, "Have you ever killed someone?" or "How many people have you killed?" I've seen veterans respond to these questions in several ways, but usually it's narrowed down to blatant honesty or responding by saying, "I don't want to talk about it." A lot of civilians don't understand that not everyone is kicking in doors and "putting boot to face." But for those of us who have been in these situations you need to be ready to respond to these inconsiderate questions.

I find the blatant honesty response is often not the best, because it makes you look like a war monger, and you either draw in the weirdos as friends from then on in, or you become marginalized by your fellow students. Death is scary to all of us, especially gentle civilians who have no concept of it. To be known as that guy who's killed someone is not a stigma you want attached to you whether or not you're proud that you did it for your country or your buddy or whatever or not.

We are a different breed and view this subject from a different viewpoint. People can't understand what they've never faced or been exposed to or experienced. The "I-don't-want-to-talk-about-it" approach makes you look more mysterious, damaged, or like a victim, and believe it or not, often draws more questions and more prying, so it's almost as if you're shooting yourself in the foot with that response.

I've found that using comedy like all of us in the military have been issued as a proper coping/defense mechanism works best. By responding with some sort of offhand joke, you can usually defuse the situation, and people will leave you alone about the subject. I usually say something stupid like "only for food" or "enough to know sex is still the best thing on the planet."

Of course you will be asked other silly questions as well like, "Oh, you were in the army? Do you know so-and-so?" Uh, come on, buddy. I think maybe out of fifty million times of being asked that question, I maybe knew three people subject to question, and I was in at least a dozen units.

Misconceptions about deployments and what Iraq and Afghanistan are really like will be topics of discussion. When I explain that Baghdad was one of the most magnificent cities I've ever seen, I'm often met with awkward looks and the response, "Isn't it just a big desert?" (These people are supposed to be educated college folk.)

You will be asked what it's like to live for ten years in an open bay barracks with forty other guys, as if you've been in basic or boot the entire time. And you will inevitably get the guy who thinks he's real smart who will gather up his buddies just to come to ask you this question, because he thinks he's going to stump you or something: "Hey man, why is the flag backward on your uniform?" Like he has some profound knowledge of flag etiquette.

Now we all know it faces that way because the military is always moving forward, never in retreat, thus it gives the impression the flag is flying. But I just simply reply to that question with, "Ah man, you know how cheap the government is. The company that made them made a bad batch and the Army is too cheap to buy us new ones, so we have to wear these backward ones."

Once again, just fight the ignorance with humor. It'll give you and your buddies an inside laugh and save you the stress of wanting to front-door kick everyone in the chest that asks you an ignorant question.

Establishing Worthwhile Professional and Social Relationships

Find role models and other veterans who have achieved what you aim to achieve. Follow them on social media and read their work. Just to reiterate what this chapter was all about: it's important to remember that during your academic career you will not be going it alone. You will be meeting and interacting with a whole network of professors and students who you are sure to see beyond the borders of your brick-and-mortar institution. You will see them not only in the business or professional world but also in the social world as well, where your reputation that you have built as a student will proceed you.

This is why it is important to establish *worthwhile* professional and social relationships. You don't just want to meet a bunch of people that you have fun partying with, although this is important too in terms of a social outlet, but you need to harbor relationships that are symbiotic—relationships that benefit you and the other.

I couldn't have asked for a better group of guys to have finished my undergraduate with. Every single one of my ROTC buddies was a stud or "studess" and helped me as much as I hope I helped them to succeed.

My first year of law school, I made the mistake of becoming buddies with the guys who were sitting on my right and left during orientation. Although it was convenient and worthwhile for the moment, it took me a year to realize these were not the guys I wanted nor needed as my allies during or after law school. I spent the rest of law school going it alone, friendly with a few people, but I spent my free time with a couple veteran locals I came to become great friends with.

Sometimes it does take time. As with a lot of things in life, trial and error makes for the best overall outcome. In the military, you have met lifelong friends, brothers, sisters, people who would literally die for you, some who have. I can't say that I have ever developed anything as close with anyone outside the military and doubt I ever will, but the potential is there for some of us.

If you're single, you need to make time for the dating scene. Like I said before, college is just as much a social education as academic. If you're married, take the time that you didn't have while you were in the military to spend more time with your family and integrate them into your education. I'm sure that they will be just as interested and supportive in what you're doing now as they were with what you were doing in the military and happy they have that much more time to spend with you.

Chapter 7

Developing a Study Program that Works for You

Everyone needs a study plan. I was always known for never having to study or being able to knock stuff out, seemingly from nothing, but the truth is, I just had a different study plan than everyone else. *No one* gets by with doing absolutely nothing. It's quite frankly impossible. Even Albert Einstein had to *learn*. The key is not letting someone else dictate your plan, because what might work for someone else might not work for you.

Do Not Let Family, Friends, Professors, or Fellow Students Dictate How You Execute Your Plan

Immediately upon entering school, whether it be undergrad, graduate, or doctoral, people are going to be up your "fourth point of contact" with their versions of what will make you successful. Don't listen to them. Hear them, but don't listen. Take the time to develop a study plan that works for you.

Maybe studying five days in advance for a test works for you fine—*do that*. Me, I would tear my hair out staring at the same stuff for five days in a row. If cramming works for you, *do that*. There is no right or wrong when it comes to studying. I learned that for some reason, probably growing up playing sports, my mind and body are at their peaks when they are put under pressure and forced to perform to their maximums; otherwise failure is sure to result.

This was key for me in the Infantry as well. Therefore, cramming has always been the best way for me to study. Some people believe that if you cram, you ultimately won't retain the information. Those are the people that cramming doesn't work for.

But don't let me dictate your study habits either. If slamming yourself in your face with your textbook like you're a Monty Python monk works for you, then *do that*. If you have to sleep on your book and learn by osmosis, do it.

I remember every professor in law school day in and day out telling us how if we weren't already studying for finals we were doomed to fail. I just laughed in my head because I knew all I needed was a day or two before the exam and I was fine. I wasn't going to jam my head all up at the beginning of the semester with stuff that didn't need to be in there.

Yet on my way out to my truck to go home there would inevitably be someone sleeping in his or her car or still in the library at night or whatever. But that's what worked for them. And guess what—we all have the same degree hanging on our walls. The point is pick a system that works for you, not your mommy or daddy or your professor or the kid sitting next to you—*you*.

Calling upon Your Military Skills to Effectuate Proper Study Habits

In order to create a proper study plan that works for you, remember your military skills: discipline, discipline, discipline. Once you find that particular study program that works, stick to it. Don't deviate or try something new because a friend of yours got a better grade. You may be setting yourself up for failure. Just fine-tune yours until you have it perfect, and if it ain't broke, don't fix it. Go back to your regimental attitude and create a "task-to-do list." Carve out study time, social time, family time, etc. All of these aspects of your life need to be incorporated into your plan in order to create effective study habits, because without downtime, you are sure to burn out.

Accomplishing the Mission

Once you have implemented a proper study plan and are in the swing of things, keep your eye on the prize. You have established relationships with professors and peers. You have learned how to deflect ignorant interactions and tolerate situations that may make you uncomfortable. You know the difference between worthwhile and unnecessary professional and social relationships. You have prepped the objective, now it's time to achieve the mission, graduation.

Chapter 8

The Importance, Pros, and Cons of Extracurricular Activities and Student Organizations

As I continue to harp on college as not just an academic education and experience but a social one as well, you need to find the time to expand your mind beyond your studies into other areas that interest you. Whether it be sports, theater, politics, or hobbies, it is integral that you do not spend your entire time with your head buried in a book.

Where you choose to go to school will dictate your options in this arena, and obviously the larger the institution, the more amount of opportunities. Deciding which clubs or extracurricular activities to be involved in can be just as important in some cases as the classes you pick. But remember the ultimate goal here is to achieve the mission by graduating, so don't let your choice in social activity eclipse your schoolwork, thus the necessity of making a pro and con list when making decisions to join certain extracurricular activities.

Fraternities/Sororities

We come from the largest fraternity in the *world*. I never fully understood the reasoning behind paying and getting paddled to make a friend but to each his or her own. Fraternities and sororities sometimes get a bad rap, but there are benefits. Oftentimes we leave the service feeling that we've left behind a brotherhood and camaraderie that we can find nowhere else, and I'm here to tell you: you won't find it anywhere else.

But many turn to fraternities and sororities as a substitute for that brotherhood and sisterhood that they miss from their time spent in the service. Frats and sororities benefit many college campuses by helping to fund on-campus functions and events through fundraisers and auctions. They support nonprofit organizations in the local community and abroad and perform community service. They also provide an esprit de corps to many colleges and are a fundamental part of some. I know the Southern schools are particularly fond of them. They can also serve as a proper place to find affordable housing and often have libraries with study materials you can utilize. Having a house full of peers can also be beneficial for study groups and just simple companionship.

A lot of us tend to draw into ourselves, believing no one can relate and, thus, become recluse and distant. This is no good for your mental health or social development—no sense in driving yourself insane by producing your own unnecessary solitary confinement.

Typically, fraternities and sororities have a rush time period in which incoming freshman and other students can attend "social functions" at their houses to get an idea of what they're all about in order to make a decision as to which one you'd like to join. Although each school does it different many schools' fraternities and sororities offer a bid to those students they would like to join, and upon acceptance of this bid, the student enters a pledge phase. This is the phase in which the student is tested in order to see whether they have what it takes to be a member of that particular fraternity or sorority. This is often where these organizations get a bad rap because of media hype about hazing and forced binge drinking, but much of this has been wrangled due to tighter college and university regulations and disciplinary measures for such actions.

All in all, you have to make the choice and see for yourself whether these organizations are worth joining. After all, there's nothing tougher than joining the military, so I wouldn't worry much. I have had both positive and negative experiences with these organizations, but my experiences have definitely grown more positive over time, which I believe is proof that the clamping down by universities through strict regulation is working.

As a public affairs officer as a second lieutenant with Temple University, I had a very positive experience in dealing with these organizations as a liaison to our ROTC unit. Together, we were able over the course of about six months to send hundreds of thousands of dollars' worth of care packages to deployed troops across the globe. So that was nice.

Sports Teams

I had the opportunity to be on a sports team in college my freshman year, and I loved every second of it, even the cutting weight part. I been an athlete my entire life, and getting the opportunity to be a college athlete was, for me, the best it was going to get.

I was lucky enough to go to a school where our coaches knew that our academics came first and wouldn't let us flounder but always remembered that I had to maintain my own self-discipline to make sure that I didn't only survive both academically and athletically but thrived.

If you do get the opportunity to play for your college team, remember that. There must be a balance. Your ultimate mission here is not to score touchdowns and take the cheerleaders home—it's to graduate with a viable degree (remember: no underwater basket weaving).

With that being said, I feel being on a sports team is the closest thing to the comradery that you feel in the military. You bleed and sweat with your teammates just like you did with your brothers- and sisters-in-arms.

If you don't receive a scholarship to play collegiate sports or have the opportunity for a walk on try-out there are other options available.

Intramural sports are huge in college, and they range all the way from ice hockey down to Frisbee football. So don't be discouraged if you don't get recruited to wrestle for Lehigh or play football for Florida State straight out of the military—you can still join a sports team and have fun.

For most of us intramural sports are more fun anyway. There's less pressure and more focus on fun than results, and ultimately they're designed more as a means to socialize than necessarily compete. So these are also a great way to make new friends, get that social interaction you're going to need so that you don't explode, and relieve stress.

Political Organizations

Most if not all of the veterans that I know who have left the military and begun and resumed their scholastic careers have become active in some sort of political organization, whether directly or indirectly.

Identifying as a Republican or Democrat and joining an organization with such title doesn't necessarily mean that you're not involved politically. There are several other organizations that you can become involved in to show your support of domestic or foreign policy. I chose to belong to the national security and law society while in law school, because it helped me bridge the gap between the military and law and also opened my eyes to an area of law I never really thought about or explored before.

Joining organizations can allow you to do just that. They do not necessarily have to define your beliefs or stance on one political issue or another but can serve as a means to educate you in that area and maybe even open your eyes to something that could eventually become your passion.

Veterans Organizations

We all know the national veterans' organizations VFW and the AL. Both offer perks and require membership fees or dues, http://www.

vfw.org/Join/Dues-Structure/. They do require that you provide proper documentation for membership, usually your DD-214, so reach into that "I-love-me book." Most universities now have student veteran's organizations that are much less formal and offer a different structure, just like any other school club. They double as social organizations and a means to be mentored by those who know what you're going through and create study groups to help you through your academic journey

Social Clubs

Every time I've ever been in trouble in my life, I've been told by my father, "You need a hobby," among other things. I always thought I had pretty fun hobbies, but I guess they were just the wrong ones.

Social clubs and organizations on campus run the gamut of the imagination. There are clubs for friggin' snail watching. And if you can't find a club you like, then create your own. I'm sure there are other people on campus who have just been waiting for someone with the fortitude to step up and say, "I want to establish a lollipop-licking club."

These are another great way for those who aren't necessarily into sports or the frat/sorority scene to seek social interaction with others and expand their educations beyond just their academic endeavors.

Just like political organizations, joining one of these can expand your mind and open it to different perspectives or likes. Or maybe you've been afraid to try something like scuba diving, and your campus offers a club that teaches you for free. Surfing clubs, glee clubs, cycling clubs—it's never ending and another great way for you to get that separation you need from the books so that you can come back at them fresh from time to time.

If you're into music, join a band. If you can't find one, start one. There is no shortage of people on campus willing to join a band—from a kazoo jamboree to a damn didgeridoo rap group, it's out there.

Utilizing Social Media

This day and age, social media is king. However, it can be the downfall of your academic and professional career. *So watch what you post.*

At the same time. it can help you stay in contact with your brothers and sisters from the service and help you to develop new relationships across campus as well as serve as a medium to yet again explore new organizations and perspectives that you may have been reluctant to explore before, all veiled in relative anonymity.

It has sparked movements across the globe such as the Arab Spring and has linked campuses across the country in order to coordinate events and organizations. It also allows you an avenue to find others like you, those you may be able to relate to like other veterans so that you can mobilize to create your own pages or on-campus organizations.

I found it helpful to me as an outlet for comic relief after a bad day. There are several veterans' websites and Facebook pages that can just make you laugh and center you back before you throat punch someone. It also allows you to follow role models, leaders, or mentors when in need of inspiration. I often check in from time to time with mentors and former leaders just to see where they are in their success and it motivates me in mine.

This is a fickle beast so be careful because although it opens your world to infinite access to information, relation, and possibilities, it can also hurt your image, both academically and professionally.

Chapter 9

Maintaining a Balance between Your Studies, Family Obligations, and Social Life

Now that you have your study plans organized, and you've had the opportunity to branch out and see what's available in terms of organizations and the social scene and have realized you have more time now for your family than you did in the military, it's time to once again prioritize.

Prioritize

Just like we made a priority list for finding a school, we have to make a priority list for your new schedule, only this one should be the same for everyone. Now this is not a priority list in terms of true priority. Rather it is time priority, so it should look like this:

> **School**: How much class time do I spend a day on campus? (Credit hours) According to the study plan that *works for me*, how many hours a day do I need to study?

Family: What are my family obligations? Does my wife or husband have work tonight and I have to watch the kids? Does my son or daughter have an event I need to attend tonight? Do I have an anniversary, birthday etc.? You get the idea. Allocation of time for family interaction, needs, and functions.

Extracurricular Activities: What clubs am I a member of? What are my responsibilities in that organization or club, sport, etc.? How much time does that take out of my day?

Establishing a Plan to Properly Allocate Time

Once you've answered these questions, you're ready to plan to properly allocate your time. Having a schedule and sticking to it rather than just flying by the seat of your pants is the difference between being stress free at school and at home and banging your head against the wall until you see Tweedy Bird. This is where we go right back to our military skill set.

Remember daily training schedules? In the civilian world we call these daily planners. Some people like them; some people don't. It's just like your study plan: you have to find what works for you.

My ex-girlfriend wrote everything in a planner, and God forbid something happened to that planner—she would implode. But as long as she had it, it was smooth sailing, and she was on track and was successful in managing her time (for the most part).

Others like to use the computer. Especially today where most college classrooms not only allow but also sometimes mandate laptops, many have decided to utilize a digital planner or calendar.

Myself, I guess call me old school: I still prefer a white board. I had my white board for school set up the same way I had it in my office in the military, divided up by day by blocks of time and simply wrote in my tasks for that particular day and time with a dry erase marker. I kept it right by my door next to my key rack so I had to look at it before I left every day. The motion of actually writing actually helps you remember as well and it helped me feel like I was still maintaining a somewhat military approach to my time management.

I always made sure to have a copy of my schedule in each of my binders as well in case I forgot one or just was having a bad day and got confused about my class routine. This will happen, so best prepare for it. You'll land on campus on a Wednesday, thinking it's a Thursday, and it'll be World War III in your head, because not only do you not have the proper stuff, but also you forget where you're supposed to be—not only in terms of your academic readiness on that particular day, but also in terms of the potential slippery slope it has on the rest of the day by affecting your family and extracurricular obligations. Go ahead and forget your wife's or girlfriend's birthday because you were too lazy to properly plan.

Still yet, everyone has a smart phone these days, so just another item we can use to manage and schedule our time to ensure our success through proper planning.

Setting Time Aside for Yourself

Now that you've got your time properly allocated for school, for your family, and for your extracurricular, you need to set some time aside for yourself. Even if it's just to sit down, drink a beer and watch your favorite show for an hour, you need some me time.

Despite the fact that all of this proper planning is designed to minimize your overall stress, having some time to yourself is necessary and will minimize it even more. If you're single, go out to the bar, go to a party, and go to a singles event. Once again, I stress the fact that this is more than an academic education, and without gaining some social knowledge and having some fun while achieving your diploma, what's the point?

One of my favorite quotes comes from a young man who I derive immense motivation from. His name is Sam Berns. Sam suffered from progeria and died in 2014. Progeria is a genetic disorder with symptoms which resemble aging manifest at a very young age. Sam was only seventeen when he died and probably had more impact on spreading the awareness of progeria than anyone to date. Sam was full of life and even knowing his inevitable fate he used to say his philosophy for life was "never miss a party if you can help it."

Chapter 10

Responding to Criticisms, Stressors, and Feelings of Being Overwhelmed

W<small>E TOUCHED ON THIS</small> earlier when we talked about answering ignorant questions, but there's a lot more to it than that. You will find yourself in situations that will irk you or piss you off, and those of you with PTSD might experience an episode or attack.

I've certainly been in my fair share of situations in the academic environment in which that "fight-or-flight" light in my head has turned on, and I have experience in making both decisions. So now I'm here to give you guidance on what is the proper response in an academic environment and how to fight the urge, the primal urge and the urge that we have been trained to respond under with a few different suggestions.

Maintaining Your Cool in Less-Than-Desirable Situations

Much like the dumb or ignorant question scenario, you'll find yourself in classroom situations where the professor or one of the students makes a remark or asks a question, oftentimes not meaning to be offensive, that may set you off.

Whether the question is directed at you or to the class or the professor usually makes no difference in my experience—they all seem to make you feel equally as uncomfortable. If no one knows you're a veteran in the class, don't be that guy or girl who has to raise his or her hand and make it known to everyone that you are. Half the time the people who do this are National Guard with no deployments on the front half of their split ops.

Most of us stay pretty low key, which means don't be that guy who comes to class with an assault pack as a backpack still rockin' a high and tight, wearing desert boots and a shirt that says "Kill 'Em All!" I'm not saying lose your identity as a veteran but spotlighting yourself never leads to a positive result. Sure I had a sticker on my laptop and wore an occasional shirt that might have given me away, but unless I told someone, no one ever really knew.

However, most of my professors knew and would from time to time call on me for my perspective, kind of outing me themselves, but it never really bothered me as I understood that in an academic environment we are *all* learning, and even though it might be a math class, you might leave having learned something having nothing to do with math.

Another skill important in this situation, which unfortunately the military did not do a good job teaching us other than the "hurry-up-and-wait" method, is *patience*. This is something that has to be developed. We're taught to believe that civilians are slow, clumsy, and lazy. They're taught that we are idiotic, brainwashed robots. Put these two animals in a room and you're in for some interesting interaction. But we know that we are held to a higher standard, and it's up to us to keep a cooler head when people say or do things that just don't make any sense.

Avoiding Conflict and Diffusing Heated Conversations

One of my first days of law school, I was sitting having lunch with a fellow classmate discussing financial aid and scholarships. Now you have to understand that I didn't necessarily fit in where I went to law school. I'm far from being a trust fund baby, and I think I was the only one who didn't drive a BMW, let alone a pickup truck. I was also the only active-duty combat veteran in the school and the only one tattooed from my neck to my feet. Needless to say I got attention, mostly negative.

What my "colleague" was trying to ask me in a nice way was "how the hell can someone like you afford to go here?" by politely asking me if the army was paying for my education. While explaining to him that I received a scholarship (awkward look) and that I was using my GI Bill, another student decided to butt into the conversation. I came to find out this was fairly common in these particular circles (the whole sticking your nose where it didn't belong business).

As I continued to explain that I was partially paying for my education through my GI Bill, the newly joined student gasped and said, "Well I don't think that's fair!" (I'm sitting in my recliner in my apartment right now while you're reading this book and I can feel your blood boil from here just like mine did right then.)

I turned around and stood up and the kid was even oblivious to threatening body language. That's when I realized half these bozos were just shootin' shit outta their mouths because they've been walking around their entire life with blinders on and a silver spoon jammed up their asses. I guess that's why they consistently spewed diarrhea from their mouths.

Now if I would have started bouncing a knife hand off his forehead and explaining to him in a rather loud tone why it was more than fair that the government *help* me with my education after what I had *helped* them with, would that have been the right thing to do? I wanted to do it. I felt like doing it. I almost did do it.

But imagine the lasting effect that would have had for the rest of the three years I would have spent at that institution. Within the first few days I would have solidified in the minds of all these people their stereotypes and clichéd thoughts of what a soldier is.

Instead I just looked at him shook my head turned around and sat back down, rubbed my ear and said *woosah*. I took it for what it was, a learning point, and I was proud of myself. I was pissed off the rest of the day, but when I got home, I went to the gym, I defused, and I sat down and did an after-action assessment.

I made the decision that, moving forward from that day on, I would have to adjust my mind-set, initiate a plan for patience, and view it like an environmental operational difference, much like when you move from one house with hostiles to a house with noncombatants. Do you treat them the same, and if you do what is the end result?

All in all, the lesson here is this will happen to you, and the way you handle it will set the tone for how you continue to handle these situations in the future, how you will be viewed by you administrators, professors, colleagues, and whether or not you will be able to achieve your mission.

Closing the Gap and Finding Common Ground

Eventually you are you going to have to interact with your classmates, both in the classroom and in social situations. You're going to be teamed up with others on projects. You're going to be required to attend certain "mandatory fun" events, etc. There is going to come a time where you are going to have to engage, close the gap, and find common ground.

Maybe you spot someone wearing a sports jersey that's your team. Maybe you've already joined a student organization ... why not volunteer to sit at the recruiting table?

Even as the dialogue in the classroom develops throughout the semester you will be able to identify those in the class who you may be able to identify with. You're going to have to start increasing your "social stock." I keep reiterating that you don't want to be that "spotlight ranger," but you don't want to be the weirdo in the back who beelines for the door when the bell rings after every class either. This isn't going to make for a fun or enlightening academic experience. Plus, you'll find that after you get past the whole "murmur-I-hate-civilians-murmur-I-wish-I-was-back-in-murmur" phase, you're going to want to open up and find common ground and establish relationships with your classmates anyway.

Understanding You Cannot Always Control the Situation: Breaking Contact

With all of this being said, you will still find that there will be situations that you simply can't avoid: that young student who was going to join the service but didn't, but he's an Eagle Scout, blah, blah, blah, who follows you around, tirelessly trying to pick your brain or try and elicit war stories from you; the hot liberal hippie (who is obviously into you) but still continues to make a point every day to fill your ear with nonsense about how you're a bad person for having served in a war motivated by the quest for oil riches; the guy whose brother's girlfriend's brother used to be a Marine; and all the other people who somehow want to genuinely engage with you but make you want to suck start your shotgun.

You will have these stressors, and rather than pop off and roundhouse kick one of their heads off or implode yourself, you're going to have to just understand that the best course of action here is just to break contact. Because once again, go ahead and get mad at the kid who idolizes you and see if that doesn't increase your social stock. Or blow up on the highly opinionated debutante and see if you don't wind up in the administrator's office.

It's just not worth it. *Break contact.*

Dealing with Stress and Feelings of Being Overwhelmed

This chapter was designed to give a few examples of anecdotes that I myself as well as some of my buddies have experienced. Hindsight is 20/20, so we can acknowledge our mistakes after they happen and try and rectify them for the future, but if we have the knowledge and tools beforehand to deal with them, well, that's all the better.

However, despite all of these we can still get stressed out from simply dealing with our daily scholarly tasks to dealing with every other aspect of the academic environment. There are times when you're going to feel overwhelmed, and I hate to say it, but not only is that the nature of the academic environment, but also that's *fucking life.*

We can choose in which ways we deal with it but those who produce negative outcomes (i.e., throwing someone off the second-story terrace) will not be conducive to us achieving our end state—graduating with a degree in a field we care about. Go out and do some PT. Go to the gym. I know that was always my favorite. (At least I could drop a weight on a civilian's foot and make it look like an accident). Go ride your motorcycle, peddle bike, whatever.

We're all trained machines, and this is just another task we have to retool our machines to perform. Every machine needs to be maintained and breaks down from time to time and needs to be oiled. So maintain yourself, and if you do see yourself breaking down, reach out, if not to someone on campus to the VA or your buddies on Facebook, family, whatever.

But just as in any mission you've ever been involved in, stress is a constant and not an excuse for failure.

Chapter 11

Making Tough Decisions: Goals v. Realities

A LOT OF TIMES, WE will tend to make goals that surpass our true realities. Although we hate to admit it, it's just a fact of life that we can't accomplish *everything* we set out to do. Whether it be because of physical limitations, time constraints, financial burdens, or other existing obligations, it's just not realistic to expect that we can take on every single task and finish it to perfection. This is life.

After I broke my back (the second time, mind you), I knew that I would never jump out of a military aircraft on active duty again. It was just a fact, even though one of my career goals was to become HALO qualified and go back to Special Forces Selection and make my career in group, it just wasn't reality anymore. My goal was no longer in line with reality.

I had to accept that, and despite my moaning and groaning about it and trying to literally sneak onto jump manifests with training units my friends were running, thinking they would look the other way and I would get away with it, it just wasn't going to happen anymore. The sooner I came to grips with it the sooner I was able to move on from it and deprioritize that as a goal and focus my efforts on the things that I could do.

This is another great quote from my man Sam who reiterates

when asked about what daily problems he faced as a result of his condition, that he doesn't focus on what he can't do but what he can.

This also applies to spreading yourself too thin when you get to college. Your main focus and main mission is to finish school and get your degree. Although I have made it clear that it is not only important but also integral to make time for your extracurricular, family, and other aspects of your life, you have to be realistic in what you can handle.

Prioritize, Prioritize, Prioritize

Once again we come back to this all-important word in the quest to succeed on the scholastic battlefield. Up to this point, this "field manual" of sorts has offered you the tools and methods with which to succeed by balancing your efforts. However, some will attempt to take on too much or spread themselves too thin and will ultimately become overwhelmed with their combined course loads, family or other obligations, and extracurricular.

Although there may be four different majors you're interested in, twenty different clubs you want to join, fifty parties or social events that week, you can't do it all. You have to prioritize this as well. You need to understand that you can't do everything, and though your military drive and initiative will tell you otherwise, it's simply not realistic.

So choose those things that are ultimately most important, interesting, and practical to your success. Join the three different clubs but prioritize their meaning to you and understand that if things become overwhelming, you may very well need to bow out of one.

Getting Out before You're in Too Deep

Which brings us to our next subject: Getting out before you're in too deep. Had I known what I know now, I would have left law school after the first semester before I was so time and financially invested.

One of the girls in my first year did just that. I spoke with her shortly after she left, thinking she'd flunked out, but she told me she'd just realized it hadn't been for her and had gotten out before she'd wasted anymore of her time or money. Now she's a doctor in New York.

Rather than looking at her as an example and reevaluating my own goals and expectations, I waited too long, and it was more practical (not necessarily beneficial) at that point for me to just lower my head and bulldoze through to the finish despite my disinterest with the entire profession halfway through my three years there.

You have to trust your gut in these circumstances. Although this may be an extreme example, this applies to all aspects of your academic career. If you're playing a sport and your grades are going downhill, you need to make a serious assessment here. Unless you're guaranteed to be playing professional athletics one day, it would probably behoove you to forgo the sports and focus on your studies.

If you hate your major and your GPA reflects that but you think you would enjoy another area of study better, *make the change*. Don't let the fear of not being able to find a job because you switch your major to something you like rather than something you believe to be practical affect your decision making in this area. Trust me: you'll be much happier and much more successful pursuing something you enjoy than something you think is going to get you a good job.

Focus on school while you're in school. Focus on getting a job when you're done. There are risks in any discipline. The demand for a safe profession like engineering may markedly decrease from the time you start school to the time you graduate, so don't rely on "safety" necessarily but opt for what you enjoy and what you know you will be successful in.

Once again, this doesn't mean take up "upside-down oil painting," or something that simply has no marketability whatsoever. And if ultimately you decide college isn't for you and you would rather go to a trade school or you're more interested in pursuing a career in a skilled trade, then *make the move*, but do it before you're in too deep.

Don't decide your junior year you want to drop out and become a plumber. At that point that's just a stupid decision. Go ahead and become a plumber after you put in one more year to at least attain the degree. At least you'll have it at that point and all the money, time, and effort you spent won't be for nothing.

Because believe me: when those student loan bills start showing up that you have to repay and you were only one year out from finishing when you decided to drop out, you'll be kicking yourself in the ass.

Developing a Proper Exfil Plan

If you do decide that college or school isn't for you and you haven't gone over the hump yet or beyond the "point of no return," which I would mark as going into your junior year, then you need a proper exfil plan.

Just like everything we've been talking about up to this point, all points of success rely on a properly executed plan. Just like the girl I told you about who left law school. She didn't just drop out and plop herself on her momma's couch, wondering what she was going to do. She was already putting a plan into motion to go to medical school before she walked out the door. She didn't skip a beat, and you can't either, for several reasons.

You'll fall into a slump, you'll start feeling like a failure and sorry for yourself and get lazy, or you'll just jump from one thing to the next and never really accomplish anything. I've seen this with people I grew up with and guys I was in the service with. They decide school isn't for them, drop out, and bounce from odd job to odd job for an indefinite amount of time, never really figuring out what they want to do. Half the time they get frustrated with a lack of sense of purpose or their financial position, do something stupid, and wind up in jail when it wasn't an issue with school but an issue with their major and their interests.

Rather than explore other options while they're still in school and have their foot in the door they fear change and insecurity in their interest and leave. Then they spend their time doing a job they don't want to do and half of them try to get back in to school once they realize what they want to do but are saddled with so much debt at that point they can't afford to go back.

Don't be that guy or girl. Stay the course. But if you do decide to leave, make sure you have a plan in place: a job lined up, another educational option, an entrepreneurial endeavor, whatever, just something so that you're not in a state of limbo that will most definitely make you even unhappier than you previously were.

Chapter 12

Using Your Experience as a Force Multiplier in the Academic Environment

Using your skills as a leader and follower developed during your time in service will be integral not only in planning, executing, and achieving your goals but also in your daily interactions with your fellow students and tackling your projects and coursework assigned by professors.

In most academic environments, especially more and more contemporarily, we are seeing a push toward peer and group projects, obviously leading to more interaction and groupthink-type learning than the traditional individual homework most of us grew up used to. There are different schools of thought on this, but nonetheless whether you agree with it, don't agree with it, hate it, or advocate for it, it's happening, and you need to be prepared.

A lot of us tend to remain withdrawn initially once we enter the academic environment, still trying to assess our environment. This is what this book is designed primarily to help you with—to provide you with supplementary tools to those you've already acquired or learned while in the service.

However, our "lead-follow-or-get-the-hell-out-of-the-way" mentality does not necessarily transfer to the academic environment as well as we would like. Oftentimes we are accused of being brash, harsh, or trying to take charge all the time, and it's true. I know that I was guilty of it, and I've seen my fellow veterans guilty of it. This is where we need to polish our otherwise abrasive techniques in this area and make them more "civilian-like."

You Are Still a Leader—Leaders Know How To Follow

One of the first things you learn upon entering the military is how to follow. Because if you can't learn how to follow, you earn yourself a real quick trip to the house. This is an important skill that most civilians never learn. They think they know, but they confuse following for hearing, and they confuse hearing for listening. So basically they let things go in one ear and out the other.

One of the biggest things I noticed about my fellow classmates is most of the time you had a conversation with them all they were doing was waiting for you to finish so they could talk; half the time they didn't even extend you the courtesy of letting you finish.

Being able to listen to someone is a skill that we have developed in the military. We take information that our leaders give us, and we apply it to accomplish the task at hand. We listen to them.

In many instances, civilians hear sounds coming out of people's mouths and then just choose to do what they were already going to do anyway—they hear them. In a group dynamic, especially in the academic environment, this can be a problem. It often leads to deadlock between group members, infighting, and unproductiveness.

So many times we are inclined to take charge. This is normal for us and really just muscle memory. If someone is indecisive, we take charge. In the military, this is great, and you likely have a commendation on your chest for some decision you've made during your career where someone failed to step up, but not in the civilian academic environment. You will be seen as a bully, a spot lighter, a teacher's pet, you name it.

We have to fall back on our abilities to be able to follow in many of these situations, and when I say follow I don't necessarily mean follow, per se, but listen. Even though half the stuff that is coming out of the mouths of your group members might be straight garbage, just listening before you jump in and take control will go a long way in helping you establish rapport with your fellow group members. They will already be expecting you to jump in and take control, so when you do, you reaffirm stereotypes and put them on the defensive.

Let them say their piece and then *tactfully* take control of the situation. A good leader knows how to be a good follower (listener) first.

Picking Your Battles

I was really bad with uniform regulations when I was in the army. When I say bad, I mean I liked to push the limits, (I always looked good—don't get me wrong. Come on now.) I liked to keep my hair and sideburns as long as possible. I bloused my pants all the way down to my ankles and walked around with my hands in my pockets. I wore my patrol cap cocked back on my head and my beret so cocked to the right it covered my right eye half the time. It was just a combination of being an SF baby and my individuality. I guess.

It was a confidence thing too. I've always been that way my whole life, pushing boundaries. My only way to "rage against the machine" that was the ultimate regimented organization in the United States.

I would get called on it constantly, and I would fight with my superiors, quoting regulations that I knew like the back of my hand specifically for that reason. The only reason I got away with it was because of my performance. If I was a shit bag, they would have sent me to the house, and I knew it and exploited it. They used to call me the barracks lawyer, ironically enough.

One day I came in to my ROTC unit wearing a black undershirt under my ACU uniform, which at one point in time was authorized in my old unit. I immediately got yelled at about it and decided, as usual, to engage and argue about it with a superior officer. (Correction: not superior but higher ranking—he was a fat piece of shit who never did anything but twiddle his thumbs over his stomach, which didn't even fit inside his uniform, and nitpick cadets about nonsensical bullshit. But I digress.)

Immediately one of the officers in the unit who I had the utmost respect for came out of his office and yelled at the top of his lungs for me to get into his office. He told me to close the door and just shook his head and said, "Are you really gonna fight with that asshole about a fuckin T-shirt? You gotta learn to pick your battles, Cubbage. Some aren't worth fighting, but you can't help but fight every one that comes your way. You fight for the sake of fighting. Go change your goddamn shirt."

And I did fight for the sake of fighting half the time. My upbringing combined with me being an infantryman straight out of combat at that point just made me that way. But he was right: I didn't always have to be right. I didn't always have to fight. Sometimes it was just better to let go and concede, because down the road there will be a more important battle to fight for which you should conserve that vigor for conflict.

Many times, just as in the service, you will run into a Mr. or Ms. Know-It-All (aka "an asshole"). Someone who already knows everything about the subject (or thinks they do), has been there done it, got the T-shirt, knee deep in shit, whatever. You're going to have to learn to deal with them just like you did in the military, only here you can't knife hand them in the forehead and tell them to shut up and make them stand at parade rest.

They will be hard to deal with—trust me. They will frustrate you, and they will make you hate the whole idea of group learning. But this is the scholarly battlefield, and this is just another obstacle you will have to overcome.

This is another area where stereotypes and clichés can be your enemy, because if you decide to jump right down this person's throat, despite the fact you know the rest of the group hates them as well, you will be the bad guy. So once again, you need to rely on your ability to tactfully engage this person and when all else fails, break contact with them.

At this point in my academic endeavors, I have learned that I simply just won't deal with these people anymore, and I just disengage and fall back into a follower role, and unless I know the person can fundamentally affect my ability to succeed, I just leave it alone. It's not worth the stress, the breath, or the effort to fight the know-it-all.

At the end of the day your mission is *your* mission; there's no sense in trying to get caught up in theirs.

Discipline Is Doing the Right Thing When No One Is Watching

I just thought it would be a good idea to remind you of this. Just in case after reading this section you may be tempted to stray from the path. Focus on your mission. Do what you need to do for *you* to succeed. Sometimes only you know that you are doing the right thing.

Chapter 13

Personal After-Action Review

After every mission in the military, we sit down and we do an after-action review or after-action assessment. This is just as important as planning the mission, as it will help you to understand what you did right, what you did wrong, and how you can revise your plan to be even more successful in the future. Ultimately the idea is that using this tool will help you to polish your plan almost to if not to the point of perfection.

This much like your study plans will be tailored to you. You can choose to do one of these at the end of every day, week, or month, whatever. It's up to you, just so long as you *do it*. This is another tool neglected by many that with diligent use proves to be a force multiplier in your success.

Taking Time to Review Your Plan and Execution

Literally sit down, decompress, grab a beer, glass of wine, Jameson, whatever you do, and grab your planner. Grab whatever other paperwork, returned assignments, study guides, returned tests/assessments you deem pertinent to the AAR. This should be a time blocked out in your schedule and should not be ignored or neglected.

For this exercise, let's use freshman year undergraduate Introduction to American Politics as a means for a monthly AAR. So it's been a month, you've had four assignments, two quizzes, one exam, and one group project, all returned and graded. You're plan for this semester was to spend two hours a night reading for the class plus another thirty minutes to complete whatever assignments you were issued. (Let's say they were short, five-hundred word essays.) You spent one hour studying for each quiz, three hours studying for your exam, and a total of five hours with your group working on your project.

You got a *pass* for each assignment.
You got Bs on both quizzes.
You got a B on your exam.
You got a B- on your group project.

Now review your plan against your goals, expectations, and your grades. Are you happy with your grades? Was the time you allotted enough to meet your goals? Do your goals meet your expectations?

Now review your execution against your goals, expectations, and grades. Did the way in which you went about studying, or where you studied affect any of these? Did the way you interacted with your group affect your group project score? You get the idea.

Do Changes Need to Be Made? Make the Reasonable and Necessary Changes

Now once you've answered these questions, do changes need to be made? I know for me that studying at home without any distractions was always best. You may find that different environments affect the way in which you study (less/more distractions, noise, etc.), which in turn changes your outcome.

Some people like to listen to music while they study or read. Some people shove fucking pillows in their ears. It's all about what works for you.

After your AAR, you should be able to identify this and make the change. If you think you could allot more time in order to raise your grades (if that's your goal, you may be happy with Bs), then do that. If you felt like you bullied your group because you had a firmer grasp on the project and this caused your group members to kind of shut down their interaction, ultimately affecting your grade, then remedy your attitude for next time.

Continue Mission

Once you've made the reasonable and practical changes, you reassess your plan, change your plan accordingly, and Charlie Mike.

Repeat

Remember to continue to do these. You may become complacent after a while or think that you don't need to do them once you've raised your grades to where they meet with your goals and or expectations. Don't stop. This needs to become muscle memory.

It's just like sports, shooting, or land navigation. These are all degradable skills, and just because you become proficient or even an expert, you don't stop taking the necessary steps that got you to your ultimate goal. This is something that you do regardless of the outcome because no matter what the end result; there is always room for improvement in some way, shape, or form. Even a sniper can shoot better with practice.

Chapter 14

End State: Using Your Experience and Education to Market Yourself in the Civilian Environment; Converting Your Military Skills to Civilian Application

Now you have the skills to properly plan, execute, and achieve your goals. You know how to interact with your professors and peers. You can interact in a group setting without taking over and you know how to assess your successes and failures and fix or correct any issues which result in you not achieving your goals. You've finally achieved your goal by graduating, and it's time to gear up toward looking passed the scholarly battlefield onto the business and professional battlefield. This will be yet another transition.

But much like basic and boot set you up for success in your military units, your school will have set you up for success in the job market. Although you have by now spent years in academia and have hopefully at this point been able to assimilate, at least to a point where you can tolerate and function in the civilian environment, you are still prior military and that is a good thing.

With all of the skills that you have learned in your academic endeavors you now have two sets of skills. Your military skills, knowledge, and education did not simply evaporate during your time in school. If anything, many of them have been honed and polished, made ready to use once again when you enter into your next occupation.

Many times, prior military members do not understand how their military skill sets transfer into civilian skill sets in the job market, me being one of them. I asked myself how I market myself in the civilian world using my military skill set when my primary job description used to be "to close with and destroy the enemy." Go ahead and tell a job recruiter that during an interview.

But we do have skills that transfer. NCOs are supervisors, officers are managers, certain skill sets directly correlate, etc. But in order to see it we have to take a step back and look at our military occupations, ranks, and knowledge through an objective lens rather than a subjective one, even though we may not want to.

A lot of us want to hold on to the prestige attached to having been an infantryman, tanker, pilot, intelligence officer, etc. But strictly speaking, these do not subjectively transfer, and we must shift our focus from holding on to titles for nostalgic purposes and transfer those into terms that civilians can understand.

Understanding that Your Military Skills and Experience Do Transfer to Civilian Jobs

For the majority of us coming out of the military, we did have jobs that directly correlate with our civilian counterparts. From engineers to linguists, military police, logistics personnel, and beyond, there is really no problem in transferring your skill sets and displaying them exactly as they would probably have read in the military.

However, those of us with combat-arms backgrounds have a bit more of a problem when it comes to trying to transfer our skill sets or even just our knowledge and expertise to the civilian sector. However, this is where we have to take that step back and remove ourselves from the persona associated with certain occupational specialties or branches and rely on our ranks or grades to relay to civilian job recruiters our credentials.

So this section will be more pertinent to those particular service members. Take for example a Marine Corps corporal machine gunner. Let's say he has now graduated with a bachelor of arts in finance, would like to work for a bank, but still wants to list on his resume his military service. Now how does this individual help a civilian job recruiter see that his military experience and knowledge as a machine gunner transfer directly to a job as a bank loan supervisor?

Well, look at the job a machine gunner must perform number one and suck anything out of that we can use:

- Responsible for $50,000+ worth of sensitive equipment
- Scored an 80+ on the GT section of the ASVAB
- Graduate of the Marine Corps Gunner School at the School of Infantry
- Proficient in mathematics in regards to ballistics and trajectory

Ok, now let's look at the rank, corporal:

- Noncommissioned officer, junior leader
- Responsible for $100,000+ sensitive equipment
- In charge of up to three marines, responsible for maintaining training standards, personnel
- Files and records pertaining to those marines
- Etc.

So now you break it down and decide what from these two categories can you take and put on your resume that the interviewer at the bank is going to care about.

They're not going to care that you qualified with a machine gun that actually may scare the shit out of them. They will care that you were responsible for and maintained in excess of $100,000 worth of equipment. They're not going to even know what a GT score is but will care that you have proficiency testing in mathematics. They will also care that you were in charge of other marines, no matter in what capacity, because the ability to manage or supervise other human beings in any setting is a transferable or marketable skill.

Now you can do this with any rank, any occupational specialty, and any job. You just have to be able to break it down and look at it from an objective standpoint. Take an infantry executive officer first lieutenant with a degree in political science who is applying for a job as a retail manager for a department store. Totally out of his wheelhouse right?

Basic Infantry Skill Set:

- Infantry officer basic course
- Weapons proficiencies across the board
- Airborne school
- Etc.

Executive Officer Specific Skill Set:

- Primary communications and logistics officer
- Responsible for $2,000,000+ worth of equipment
- Responsible for vehicle, weapons, and facilities maintenance
- Responsible for designing daily training schedules and facilitating all supply orders and allocations, etc.

Ok, now the rank of first lieutenant:

- Second in command of a company in charge of 150–250 men
- Proficient in platoon size and company tactical and strategic operations
- Etc.

So now this guy has no business in terms of his degree managing a Macy's, but if he so chooses, how does he tailor his skill set to make him marketable to a hiring agent looking for a retail manager?

Dump all the infantry-specific stuff. Macy's don't care high speed. (Sorry—don't get butt hurt.)

Now look at the job of the executive officer specifically. "Responsible for over $2,000,000 worth of equipment" translates right into merchandise in this situation. "Responsible for facilities maintenance … responsible for training schedules" translates easily into employ work schedules and responsible for supply orders an allocations speaks for itself. It's a logistics job.

Then the rank, "second in command responsible for up to 250 men," that's a lot of dudes or "dudesses." This shows the recruiter this individual can manage a high volume of employees.

And, lastly, "proficient in strategic operations." This translates to the civilian job world directly to mean overall operations much like it does in the military.

So it's easy to see how you can cherry-pick your military experience, knowledge, occupational skills, as well as the responsibilities afforded your rank and grade, to translate them directly to be objectively viewed as civilian workplace marketable skills.

Combining Your New Education and Prior Service into a Marketable Package

Once you achieve the goal of attaining your degree, you are a double threat. Now not only do you have the same degree that your academic peers have, but also you have your military experience to boot. (No pun intended.)

This is highly attractive to employers and shows that you know how to get the job done. It screams initiative and discipline, and many employers are happy to know they are hiring someone who quite possibly will be easier to train and more mature in their overall professional behavior, not to mention being a veteran helps you get a leg up on civilian counterparts when applying for civil service jobs and makes you an affirmative action higher for other civilian employers.

Some veterans chose to forgo listing their military service on their resumes when applying to civilian jobs for fear that their skills won't transfer, they may appear intimidating, or they simply don't know how to tailor their resume to properly display how their given skills do transfer. I think I've shown in the last section that this is quite easy to accomplish once you do the simple break down and cherry picking necessary to make it look more objective. Having your military service combined with your new education is an extremely marketable package, and you should not forgo listing your military service for fear that it may marginalize you.

That is not to say that I haven't seen it intimidate employment recruiters before and have heard stories from friends of mine who have issues explaining during interviews how their military service would be marketable, but these are few and far between and can usually just be chalked up to ignorance on the interviewer's part.

Chapter 15

Interviews, Resumes, and Cover Letters

The Importance of a Properly Designed Resume

OVER EVEN JUST THE past three years, I have seen the acceptable forms of resumes change three or four times. But I will say that every resume must include at least two things: education and professional/work experience.

I've included a sample resume that seems to be the acceptable form for the time being and has been the format that I've used for years at the end of this book. But most formats are pretty much the same. Contact information at the top. Education listed in chronological order next.

You will want to list any awards, scholarships, grants, organizations, etc., under each institution you list here. I would also list my GPA if it's above a 3.5.

The next section will consist of your professional/work experience. Some people use the word history instead of experience, but I think experience sounds more professional. Whether you use the word "professional" or "work" will also depend on where you've worked. If you worked at TGI Fridays, I probably wouldn't list that as professional experience unless you were the manager, just like I wouldn't list working as a stock broker for Merrill Lynch as simply "work experience."

I usually add another category at the end, professional awards and organizations. Here you can list whether you belong to the VFW or the FOP and whether or not you've received any awards or accolades during your professional career. Sometimes this can be beneficial; sometimes recruiters just don't care. It really all depends. This is one of those areas where there really is no exact science.

They should, however, be no more than two pages long. So make sure you prioritize (there's that word again) what really needs to be on there. There are several professional resume review sites that offer to write your resume for a fee or review and revise what you've already written for a fee. I have dealt with several of them just for shits and giggles, and every single one of them contradicted the other ones.

The VA has programs that can help you with this. Your school will have a career center that will help you as well. It's been my experience that they are the best in terms of being up-to-date with the format local employers are looking for, because they deal with them directly on a daily basis. So if in doubt I would trust the opinion of your institutions career center over all else.

However, absolutely do not wing it. A shitty resume will label you right off the bat as a turd and will likely end up in the shred pile before it's even read.

Developing Multiple Resumes for Multiple Applications

Different industries and different jobs also have different formats they expect or are used to. You're not going to send the same resume to a bank for a loan officer position that you're going to send to a military contractor for a mobile personal security detail position. The focus on the format won't necessarily be what you need to consider, rather the content.

Just like earlier where you tailored your military experience to be more objective in the eyes of prospective civilian employers who don't want to nor would understand military jargon, acronyms, or specialty skill sets, you may want to have other resumes that do get more specific or subjective that you can send to companies that may be a little bit more savvy in those areas or specialties.

Designing a Cover Letter that Reflects You; No More Cookie-Cutter Crap

A cover letter lets a particular company or position you're applying for know why you want to work for them specifically and what you bring to the table uniquely. There are cookie-cutter cover letters you can attach to your resume when sending them out that simply give a brief overall about how you're "a high-speed, low-drag, dynamite bad ass," but most companies look right past these.

Tailor your cover letter to the position you are seeking. It's been my experience that a lot of companies really don't care about cover letters, but that all depends on what industry you are in. The law community gets off on them. Law firms love to hear about themselves and why it is you want to work for them so bad, and I'm sure it's the same in some other industries as well.

So do what you have to do, "fake the funk" if you have to, but if a company does require a cover letter, don't blow it off because they're likely to blow you off.

Interviewing Techniques; Using What You've Learned from Promotion Boards to Establish a Successful Interview Strategy

For those of you who have been through promotion boards, which I would imagine would be the bulk of those reading this book, you know what it's like to be in the hot seat. Military Promotion Boards are obviously much more formal and are geared more toward assessing your confidence level, proficiency in your job, and ability to lead troops. Civilian job interviews tend to be much less formal and focus more on your prior job experience and ability to perform (or at least be trainable) the job you're applying for.

However, as many differences as there are, there are similarities. Just like a military promotion board, in a civilian job interview you are being assessed, judged, scrutinized, and measured as soon as you walk in the door. From your appearance, to your mannerisms, the way you talk and interact initially with the interviewer, your handshake, and even the way you sit in the chair, you are being interviewed.

For most of us who have been in the military, civilian job interviews are not intimidating and are typically a breeze, as long as we are prepared. You should always have at least a nice folder with three copies of your resume in it and a pen and legal pad or notebook with you.

Depending on the job you are being interviewed for will dictate your dress code, but usually a suit and tie for males and pantsuit or skirt for females in any professional environment is appropriate. However, you do not want to show up for a job as a janitor in a tuxedo. Just remember back to *Step Brothers* and think how silly they looked during their interview.

I actually interviewed once for a job where the daily dress code for employees was khakis and a button-down or polo. I showed up in a suit and tie, and I think they thought I was there to audit their books. Bottom line, you really can't go wrong with a suit, but I would do a little research into the company, position, and responsibilities before you show up either too formal or not formal enough.

JOE SNUFFY
123 Crazy Lane, Fort Lauderdale, FL 33316
(954) 123-1234
jsnuffy@us.army.mil

EDUCATION

FLORIDA ATLANTIC UNIVERSITY, Davie, Florida
Finance, May 2016

Awards & Honors:	GPA 3.8, 2016
	Dean's List, 2012–2016
Activities:	FAU Veterans Organization, President, 2016
	Phi Kappa Alpha, Treasurer, 2013–2016
	Intramural Soccer, 2012–2016

WORK EXPERIENCE

FIRST FINANCIAL BANK, Fort Lauderdale, Florida
Loan Officer Student Intern, 2016
- Shadowed loan officer and kept accurate notes
- Aided loan officer in developing and processing loan applications
- Greeted new bank customers and maintained a professional appearance and welcoming attitude in order to promote and keep business
- Prepared excel spreadsheets to keep track of new customer trends

PUBLIC HOUSE, Fort Lauderdale, Florida
Head Bartender/Server, 2013–2016
- Tended Bar and provided exemplary customer service to patrons
- Responsible for opening and closing restaurant, entrusted with keys and access to tills
- Conducted nightly money counts for all bartenders
- Responsible for supervising morning layouts and nightly cleanups

BIG LOTS, Davie, Florida
Security Guard, 2013
- Conducted security checks of parking lot and outside surrounding area
- Conducted security checks of interior of store, kept accurate log of checks
- Prevented loss by checking bags alerting store alarms
- Provided professional appearance and presence to deter theft
- Monitored video surveillance in order to spot suspected theft threats
- Kept the store a safe place by mediating and conflicts or disputes

UNITED STATES ARMY, DELTA COMPANY 1-10 INFANTRY, Fort Hood, Texas
Specialist, Infantry Team Leader 2009–2012

- Responsible for four infantry soldiers, training, and personnel records
- Conducted morning physical training and monitored development of team progress
- Conducted firearms training and qualification for team
- Kept files and conducted developmental counseling of all soldiers in team
- Responsible for all team sensitive equipment worth in excess of $100,000
- Qualified in Microsoft Office, Excel, Word, PowerPoint, Outlook

COMMUNITY SERVICE, ASSOCIATIONS

Wounded Warrior Project Alumni, Veterans of Foreign
Wars Member, Volunteer Soccer Coach

(Contact Information)
Joe Snuffy
Crazy Lane
Fort Lauderdale, Florida 33316
954-124-1234(c)
jsnuffy@us.army.mil

(Address and name of company and department hiring)
Human Resources, Recruiting and Hiring, Loan Department
Gold Coin Bank and Trust
1234 Beach Road, Suite 300
Jacksonville, Florida 32256

(Salutation—use the name of the person if you know. If not, then sir or madam is appropriate)
Dear sir or madam,

("Introduction"—where you found the job, brief explanation of why you want the job, short intro)
Your online employment site has advertised an opportunity for employment as a loan officer supervisor. I am not only qualified to perform but also extremely enthusiastic about it. I am a recent graduate of Florida Atlantic University where I graduated summa cum laude with a bachelor of arts in finance. While there I excelled in the areas of mathematics and financial studies. I was selected to participate in a selective summer student internship with First Financial Bank of Fort Lauderdale, a leader in the industry. While there I met Johnny Smith who directed me to your website ...

("The Pitch"—What do you bring to the table, skills and qualifications *relevant* to the job?)
My skills as an experienced team leader in the United States Army Infantry have prepared me for any task and have provided me with discipline, drive, and determination ... (Go on about attributes important for the position and how they parallel to the job as a team leader and then talk about your education and the skills you gained during your internship that apply directly to the position. You want to *interpret* your resume here. Do not simply just restate it. Talk about how the skills or "bullet points" on your resume are relevant to the position you are applying for. You can even talk about your time as a head bartender where you were in charge of the house money, anything relevant in your resume that applies to *this particular job*.)

(The "kiss-ass" closing)

I thank you for your time and consideration in this matter and hope we can find a position for me at Gold Coin Bank and Trust. I would love nothing more than to be able to work for your organization in as a Loan Officer Supervisor. I believe in your mission and hope I can help you fulfill it.

Respectfully and sincerely,

Joe Snuffy

Conclusion

I THINK YOU NOW POSSESS the supplementary skills to those you have already learned throughout your military career to be successful in your transition into the academic environment. I know much of this may have seemed redundant, but that's for a reason. Much like in the military, we train, train, train, and train some more to be ready for when we have to go to war.

I've used a lot of metaphors and analogies throughout this book to try and make it more readable for you and to make it feel more military than civilian in its context. I think that is what is necessary to help relay these concepts to you in order for you to attain maximum comprehension and success.

I've said it multiple times throughout this book that I wish I had something like this to read before I left the military and went back to school, and I mean that 100 percent. It wasn't easy for me in many ways. I actually fought the transition, and I know it won't be easy for many of you in many ways, and you will also fight, so I only hope that I have tackled many of the concerns that you may have in entering the scholarly battlefield.

I've done my best to answer the questions asked by many of my friends and soldiers who prompted me to finally sit down and write this book, so I pray that it will help everyone else who reads it as well. Provided in this book now are the resources you need in order to be able to properly transition out of the military and into the academic environment. Not only have I provided with you with the academic resources, but also I have given you the personal resources in order to be successful. If you follow the guidelines and keep on top of your health, budget, priorities, and personal issues there is no excuse for failure.

I now call on you to make the decision to take this next step in your life and set out to achieve higher education. Once again, I applaud you. You can do it. We've all been through hell and back, the most of us, and this is just another assignment. So good luck, God speed, and I'll see you on the other side.

Sources

GI Bill Information
https://www.gijobs.com/difference-between-the-post-9-11-gi-bill-and-montgomery-gi-bill/

SAT Information
https://www.collegeboard.org/

LSAT Information
http://www.lsac.org/

MCAT Information
https://students-residents.aamc.org/applying-medical-school/taking-mcat-exam/prepare-mcat-exam/

GRE Information
http://www.ets.org/gre/

GMAT Information
http://www.mba.com/us

Department of Veterans Affairs
http://www.va.gov

Joint Service Transcripts
https://jst.doded.mil

There are also plenty of fun ones designed for comic relief, which I will leave you to find on your own as that is part of the fun—the process. Several are blogs you can find generally, while others are Facebook pages that I'm sure many of you are aware and belong to already.

About the Author

MIKE IS A COMBAT veteran and native of Philadelphia who comes from a long line of military service. He enlisted in the United States Army Special Forces Recruit Program in 2003 during the height of the war in Iraq. The majority of his enlisted career was spent with the famous 101st Airborne Division, and in 2005, Mike deployed to Baghdad, Iraq, in support of Operation Iraqi Freedom, where he served as an infantry team leader and squad designated marksman and was recognized as both the Soldier of the Month and Soldier of the Quarter. Upon his return, Mike was chosen as the honor graduate of the Third Infantry Division Noncommissioned Officer Academy and was recommended by his command to compete for a slot in a competitive program designed to turn noncommissioned officers into commissioned officers.

In 2009 Mike was commissioned as a second lieutenant where he served as an officer recruiter and public affairs officer and subsequently served out the majority of his officer career on Sand Hill, Fort Benning, "Home of the Infantry," as the executive officer for an Infantry Basic Training Company.

Mike holds a bachelor of arts in political science and foreign policy from Temple University, a master of arts in international relations and conflict resolution with a concentration in international and transnational security issues from American Military University, and a juris doctor in US law from Nova Southeastern University Shepard Broad Law School. Mike has also published articles for the

Philadelphia Metro magazine and the *Florida Public Interest Journal.* He is a founding member and was the inaugural keynote speaker for the Temple Veterans Day Committee, speaker and panelist for the Nova Law Symposium on Post Traumatic Stress Disorder, and an inaugural member of the Nova Law Veterans Law Clinic.

101 GETS IT DONE